Perfect

Perfect

The Rise and Fall of John Paciorek,
Baseball's Greatest One-Game Wonder

STEVEN K. WAGNER

BREAKAWAY BOOKS
HALCOTTVILLE, NEW YORK
2015

ISBN: 978-1-62124-016-7
Library of Congress Control Number: 2014916480

Published by Breakaway Books
P.O. Box 24
Halcottsville, NY 12438
www.breakawaybooks.com

Cover photo courtesy of the Houston Astros

FIRST EDITION

Contents

For Jesus.
For my parents, who encouraged;
For Michelle and Hannah, who supported;
And for Peter, who died too young. *Requiescat in caelum.*

Foreword

Albie Pearson

(Albie Pearson, American League Rookie of the Year in 1958, played nine seasons in the major leagues. His best season was 1963, the year of John Paciorek's perfect game, when he hit .304, was named to the American League All-Star team, and finished fourteenth in the league's Most Valuable Player balloting.)

The late Branch Rickey, a baseball visionary whose legacy as an executive rests comfortably in Cooperstown, spoke percipiently when he said, "It is not the honor you take with you, but the heritage you leave behind."[1] Across the generations, baseball has established a unique heritage built upon the legacy of earlier generations and launched by the many fine players who have helped make the sport the rich institution it has grown to become. That roster swells with excellence and includes such immortals as Christy Mathewson in the early 1900s, Babe Ruth in the 1920s, Lou Gehrig in the 1930s, Stan Musial in the 1940s, Mickey Mantle in the 1950s, and Sandy Koufax in the 1960s. The catalog of baseball's high achievers certainly continues on after that, although my firsthand observations as a player do not. No matter—when it comes right down to the spirit of the game itself I am confident that as a national pastime, baseball will always be baseball.

As a former player I remember the 1960s with wonderful fondness and a keen sense that we were witnessing a special chapter in baseball history. Who could forget the great Roger Maris and his gracious effort to eclipse Babe Ruth's single-season home run mark, a chase that ended on the final game of the 1961 season when Maris hit No. 61 over the right-field fence at Yankee Stadium? Or Don Drysdale's six consecutive shutouts in 1968, a mark that has stood the test of time? Or the 1969 New York "Miracle" Mets, a team that sprang from rags to capture World Series riches following the club's establishment in 1962 as one of the worst teams in baseball history? Through the up-and-down, sometimes disordered world of major-league baseball, two things have remained constant: the consistently outstanding quality of ballplayers and their dogged pursuit of excellence, which during the turbulent 1960s provided the country with a welcome daily diversion—and lots of good, clean fun.

Not all players pursue excellence in quite the same way. One who uniquely found it was John Paciorek (pronounced *puh-SHORE-ick*), a big-league ballplayer who on one special day in baseball history achieved far more than even he might have imagined possible: baseball immortality. Others have reached their own pinnacles of achievement, but few of them played the game for so short a duration as John. Do I remember John and his perfect game? I do not, and therein lies the paradox: Most people don't. That doesn't minimize his unique accomplishment or the hero that he represents to the many young ballplayers striving to reach a lofty goal: a position on a major-league roster. John is the impetus to persist for every child who ever told his father, "I want to be a baseball player." He's an icon for every athlete who ever remarked, "I'd give anything to play in the major leagues for just one day." He's the autograph on the glove that every boy wants to represent—the imagined face on a baseball card in our spokes, held tightly by a clothespin built of dreams. That John Paciorek accomplished his "feat of dreams" is remarkable in itself and a testament not only to his athleticism, but also to his persistence, tenacity, and sheer devotion to a game he loved to play. And, of course, to the perfect timing that presented him with a rare opportunity to rise to the big leagues on Sunday, September 29, 1963, for on any other day it might not have occurred. As any ballplayer knows, and as John himself learned on that special day, opportunity and the ability to recognize and seize it are a road map to success—no matter how short-lived that success may be.

In professional baseball, players come and go, some achieving short bursts of success, others carving out long and magical careers. Although half a century later many people remain unacquainted with John and his day of distinction, that doesn't diminish his stature; that he played the game and played it to the best of his God-given ability *does* matter. For when all was said and done, when the dust around home plate had drifted toward the Colt Stadium grand-stands, when the chalk that marked the base paths had been scuffed by anxious cleats into fine clumps of gray dirt, John was as much a part of the fabric of major-league baseball as Mathewson or Gehrig or Ruth. The brevity of his career by no measure disqualifies him for that.

For those who are strangers to John this book will serve as an introduction. John was a peer, a man who played for an expansion team at the same time I was playing for an expansion team half a continent away. To my knowledge we never met. We never played against each other. We were, you could say, disacquainted brothers in a timeless fraternity of men who comprise the totality of major-league baseball across the ages, men with the spirit of young boys who played the game as grown-up boys and who, in many cases, retired from the game without ever crossing paths with those whose statistics we perused nearly every morning in the "other league" box scores.

John's time in the spotlight came and went far too quickly. Had he not suffered a debilitating injury it's safe to assume he might have had a long and glorious career, bringing joy and entertainment to hundreds of thousands of fans in National League ballparks around the country. That it didn't work out the way he might have hoped or envisioned is a disappointment—but there's no shame, certainly not on John. During the brief time that was ordained to him as a major leaguer he played as well as any man could have, given the physical tools he was blessed with and the pain that afflicted him. In the end he was a victim of injury, like so many outstanding baseball players before him. Players like Dizzy Dean, whose great career was short-circuited by a line drive that broke his toe, causing him to alter his pitching motion and thus damage his arm. And Mark "The Bird" Fidrych, whose limitless potential, soaring popularity, and on-field unconventionalities were stilled by a torn rotator cuff after just five seasons. The difference between John and others is the speed with which his light was extinguished. It shone brightly for only one game, for a moment, then went dark. He lasted just three hits and a few times around the bases. However, he left a footprint on the game of baseball that has only enlarged as time has passed and his achievement has emerged from the shadows—if it has yet fully emerged.

To put John's success in perspective, he drilled more hits in his first and only major-league game than Babe Ruth did during his short first season, which spanned five games. He notched more RBI than Jimmy Foxx did during his initial abbreviated season, when he played in ten games. And, he scored as many runs as Ernie Banks did in thirty-nine games during his final season of major-league ball.

John was a baseball player, and a very good one. His heritage, one that remains deeply etched on the game more than fifty years after he "retired," is one of skill and grace and resolve, and he sets an example for anyone who might hope to play the game at the highest possible level. The message of this book is unmistakable: While perfection in life is never attainable, perfection in baseball *is* within reach—at least in the short run: over an inning, or perhaps a game. John showed us that. For John, there would be no long run, so he had to make the short run count.

Over the years many pitchers have thrown perfect games. And while hitters strive for that same excellence, John Paciorek's is the finest example of a perfect one-game career, neatly packaged, the quotient of his own perfect afternoon of hitting, fielding, and base running that baseball has ever seen. Indeed, John's perfect day is one for the ages . . . and a baseball story worth telling.

Prologue

[A box score] doesn't tell how big you are, what church you attend, what color you are, or how your father voted in the last election. It just tells what kind of baseball player you were on that particular day.
—*Branch Rickey, baseball executive*

My interest in baseball's one-game wonders began in 1980, long after I had relinquished my Clete Boyer glove to the childhood treasures heap in our suburban Los Angeles home and shortly after leaving United Press International, where I'd covered sports, among other things, for the international wire service's Boise, Idaho, bureau. I had resigned from UPI to accept a position as suburban bureau chief with the *Portland Oregonian*, and one day while browsing at a bookstore near downtown Portland I purchased a copy of *The Baseball Encyclopedia*, which at that time weighed in at six and a half pounds and proclaimed itself, unequivocally, "The complete and official record of major league baseball." The book is certainly a thorough, thoughtful, and well-researched compendium of statistics and other vital major-league information: everything you always wanted to know about the sport but wouldn't have time to learn through independent research. While strumming through its endless pages of eye-straining type, my interest was drawn to an obscure society of ballplayers, men who for reasons lost to the ages played in one—and only one—major-league baseball game. In each instance there was no explanation why these men abruptly came and went, just a line of numbers that when extrapolated gave only a scant summary of what each player did at the plate, in the field, or on the mound on that singular day in each of their lives. The quick demise of such obviously talented players, who for only a moment, a heartbeat, a tick in time, if you will, rose to the pinnacle of a sport that demanded both great skill and undying commitment, was simply left to the imagination.

Perhaps Willie Stargell of the Pittsburgh Pirates described the challenge of baseball best: "They give you a round bat and they throw you a round ball and they tell you to hit it square," he said.[2] That's the essence of baseball, and it takes enormous skill to succeed, to climb to the height of a sport so incongruous that it makes you hit a round object with another round object—sometimes thrown at more than a hundred miles an hour. The men in this elite but little-known group obviously had what it takes to succeed, to put round on round or to throw round past round—so what happened to them? Why, after succeeding so brilliantly, did they fail to catch on permanently as so many others did before and after them? There seemed to be no clear answers to the question, only numbers, more numbers, and more questions.

For me, a statistic guy with a fair imagination, that wasn't good enough. Why, I wondered, did Boston Braves pinch hitter Steve Kuczek go 1 for 1 in 1949, finishing his major-league debut with a double and a perfect 1.000 batting average—never to play again? Why did catcher Charlie Lindstrom go 1 for 1 with a triple and an

RBI for the Chicago White Sox in 1958, then disappear forever? Why did Katie Keifer win his only major-league game for the 1914 Indianapolis Hoosiers, pitching a complete game and allowing just two runs? And what about Earl Huckleberry, who won the only major-league game he would ever play in for the 1935 Philadelphia Athletics, pitching six and two-thirds innings—then became a memory? For these and other players there were no obvious explanations—only lingering questions.

The reasons why myriad other major-league ballplayers failed to make the grade, those who had no further success, who never threw another pitch or swung another bat in the big leagues, were more obvious. Players like Frank Wurm, who hung up his spikes after pitching in one game for the 1944 Brooklyn Dodgers, recording a painfully high earned run average of 108. (His last name probably didn't help much, either.) And starting pitcher Len Gilmore, 0–1 with a 7.88 ERA in an eight-inning stint with the 1944 Pittsburgh Pirates. The list of ballplayers who, like Wurm and Gilmore, failed to impress either their managers or the owners when given their one shot at a major-league career, or who for some other reason never played again, was not insubstantial.

Others played magnificently when called upon to perform at the highest level of professional baseball: right fielder Jackie Gallagher, 1 for 1 with an RBI for the 1923 Cleveland Indians. Never played again. Catcher Red Lutz, 1 for 1 with a double for the 1922 Cincinnati Reds. Gone. Catcher Ralph "Curly" Onis, 1–1 in his only game with the 1935 Dodgers. Ditto.

Still others, now better known, mysteriously disappeared, then reinvented themselves several years later and reappeared on the baseball scene, becoming icons in another iteration. Playing under famed manager Casey Stengel, shortstop Raoul "Rod" Dedeaux (he was so forgettable that the 1988 edition of *The Baseball Encyclopedia* incorrectly spelled his name *Dedaux*), a teammate of Onis, went 1 for 4 in his only major-league game for the 1935 Brooklyn Dodgers, abruptly disappeared, then was hired to manage the University of Southern California baseball team seven years later. Many years after his inauspicious major-league debut Dedeaux turned USC into a perennial baseball powerhouse, guiding the Trojans to ten National Collegiate Athletic Association titles during a forty-five-year career that ended in 1987.

In 1936 first baseman Walter Emmons Alston, who became better known to Brooklyn and Los Angeles Dodgers fans as Walt Alston, also appeared in only one major-league game, going 0 for 1 with a strikeout and a sacrifice while playing for the St. Louis Cardinals. As a player he, too, faded into the one-game career netherland, only to later manage the Brooklyn and Los Angeles Dodgers to four World Series championships. Alston, known as Smokey during his years with the Dodgers, is widely regarded as one of the finest major-league managers ever to wear a baseball uniform; he was elected to the Baseball Hall of Fame in 1983, the year before he died.

Over the following year I combed through all 2,875 pages of *The Baseball Encyclopedia*, searching for similar success—and failure—stories. Through it all one name stood out above all others: John Francis Paciorek, who as a member of the Houston Colt .45s went 3 for 3 with three RBI, four runs scored, and four errorless plays in the outfield—including two fine catches for putouts—on the final day of the 1963 season; he never again played at the major-league level, prompting Jim "The Toy Cannon" Wynn, who went 1 for 3 as a twenty-one-year-old rookie playing alongside Paciorek that day, to remark, "He's one of a kind."

Paciorek's performance piqued my curiosity, although not enough to lay aside my regular work and pursue some answers until more than a decade later.

By 1991 I had left the *Oregonian* and was working as a freelance journalist near Los Angeles. With time occasionally on my hands in between writing assignments, and once again becoming curious about these one-game stars, I set about trying to track down Paciorek. Unfortunately, I knew only the name of his better-known baseball brother, Tom, who had played for my hometown Dodgers when I was a young man; which team John had played for (Houston); his hometown (Detroit); and the few impressive numbers he had put together during the only major-league game in which he would ever play.

Employing a bit of journalistic sleuthing and some strategically selected telephone directories, I was able to locate Paciorek living in Southern California and working at the Clairbourn School in San Gabriel, California, just seventeen miles from my home. Becoming more curious as the man's story came within reach, I dialed the telephone.

A friendly, unassuming man, Paciorek was polite when we spoke on the phone, although not overly enthusiastic about the prospect of being interviewed for an article—nor was he surprised that I, a freelance writer, was interested in talking with him about his abbreviated "career." Perhaps it was diffidence, or simply a failure to regard his short stint as a major-league player as anything special in the scheme of things, a fact he alluded to in his book: *The Principle of Baseball: And All There Is to Know About Hitting*, published in 2012.

While the book focuses mostly on baseball technique—the mechanics and intricacies of hitting and throwing a baseball, skills that as a right fielder he knew plenty about—and contains only a few references to himself, Paciorek did ascribe authority to the tract by describing himself as "the only player in baseball history to bat 1.000 and sole possessor of the highest on-base and slugging percentages." He then portrayed hitting a baseball as "not as hard as some people make it [out] to be," but "a lot harder than most people want it to be."[3]

Perhaps that self-diminution, if one could call it that—if it's not that hard then why did he last only one game?—explains why Paciorek's home on the outskirts of Los Angeles displays few mementos from either The Game or from his minor- or major-league tenures. He appears, simply, not to regard his performance as the Sisyphean achievement it truly was. Or does he? In his book he presents his thesis on hitting a baseball:

> Ted Williams said it best for all of us who have ever played the game of baseball [or] participated in other forms of athletics: hitting a baseball is the single most difficult thing to do in all of sports. No other individual sport skill encompasses the variety of challenging variables that a batter has to put in order to be a proficient hitter. It takes physical strength, flexibility, quickness and timing as well as the mental attributes of courage, confidence, determination and fortitude for even the least skilled professional to stand in against a 95 mph fastball or an 85 mph slider.[4]

Despite what I perceived as reluctance to tell his unique story,

Paciorek was polite enough to sit and talk with me for as long as I wanted. When he talked about baseball, he knew the game from the fundamentals of hitting to the fundamentals of catching and throwing. I was asking him to talk about a sport he loved, so I reasoned— why wouldn't he be willing to talk?

The interview took place on January 23, 1991, at Clairbourn School, with a short photo session afterward on the modest bleachers situated next to the sprawling field where he coaches the school's athletic teams.

Located just east of Los Angeles, south of Pasadena, and across town from the Mission San Gabriel that Father Junipero Serra founded in 1771, Clairbourn is a parochial academy where Paciorek has taught for more than thirty-five years. It is situated near Huntington Drive, a main thoroughfare that parallels California 210, which connects Pasadena with Colton (a community that will become important later on) and points east. On the day I interviewed him Paciorek was amicable, patiently answering all of my questions for about two hours.

My story ran prominently in the *Los Angeles Times* on January 31, 1991. It marked the first such piece written about Paciorek's short career, and it opened the floodgates. The *Times* followed up that article with a similar piece on Paciorek a decade later, underscoring the newspaper's continuing interest in the man and his unusual achievement, and *Sports Illustrated* ran a lengthy story on him in July 2012. An Internet search of his name turns up dozens of interviews, short articles, and other references to Paciorek, describing his one-game career in what minimal detail there is but offering little in-depth information about the man himself.

Despite Paciorek's newfound popularity, many questions remain:

Why does he not regard his accomplishment as highly as others do? How good was Paciorek and how good might he have become? How did his baseball prowess compare with that of his younger brothers, Tom and Jim (Jim played one season in the American League, slugging two home runs, knocking in ten runs, and batting .228)? And how, if at all, did his brief flirtation with major-league baseball set the compass for what he would accomplish later in his life—author, educator, and mentor to others in his immediate and extended families, including sons Pete and Mack, who later attempted careers in baseball but failed to achieve the pinnacle that Paciorek did?

Tom Paciorek, in a 1991 telephone interview with me shortly after I interviewed his brother John, shed some light on at least one of those questions: how good his older brother really was or could have been if his career had played out a little differently. Describing the brevity of his brother's major-league career as, in a word, "sad," then speaking with a twinge of bitterness in his voice, he discussed John's skills, abilities, and potential in brief, but unmistakable, terms. His voice rose noticeably in volume as he spoke: "He was much better than I was," said Tom, who years later told a sportswriter, "He was a great prospect—he had unbelievable power. He can reflect on that one day and be very happy."[5] He should know. At six foot four and 215 pounds, Tom hit .326 with fourteen home runs and sixty-six RBI for the Seattle Mariners in 1981, finishing tenth in the balloting for Most Valuable Player that season. Tom also made his only All-Star game appearance that year (he went 1 for 1 with a single and has a lifetime All-Star game batting average of—what else?—1.000.), competing on the field with future Hall of Famers Tom Seaver, Steve Carlton, Nolan Ryan, Rollie Fingers, Goose Gossage, Rod Carew, and Reggie Jackson. He hit over .300 four times in his long career and retired in 1987 with a lifetime batting average of .282—respectable by today's standards, and numbers that nowadays would earn him significant financial compensation.

Then there was brother John.

"He could have had a long major-league career," Tom said of his brother. Period.

Instead, John Paciorek had a short major-league career. Still hurting the following season, Paciorek had difficulty both hitting and throwing and failed to make the Colt .45s' opening-day roster. Understandably disappointed in light of their right fielder's brilliant debut on the last day of the 1963 season, the team sent him to their Class A Durham Bulls team in the Carolina League, then to the Class A Statesville Colts in the Western Carolinas League.

"I was terrible," Paciorek said of his 1964 spring training performance in Cocoa Beach, Florida. "I did nothing."

He added, "I depended solely on my reflexes: I would watch the ball, then hit the ball. I had no idea how to hit correctly. I knew I could no longer depend simply upon my strength."

From spring training forward it was all uphill, with Paciorek playing for little-known teams like the Batavia Trojans, the Asheville Tourists, and the Rock Hill Indians, until he exited baseball for good in 1969 at the age of twenty-four. Just six years after his amazing single-game performance, one that continues to astound, Paciorek was watching games from his living room couch while former teammates Rusty Staub, Joe Morgan, Jim Wynn, and others were making names for themselves as career major leaguers.

This book attempts to appraise the significance of Paciorek's accomplishment that day in 1963—half a century ago: how he achieved a moment of glory in the unusual way that he did, what the game means today both to him and to others, and, more important, whether his single-game career mark—like Johnny Vander Meer's consecutive no-hitters and Cy Young's 511 career wins—is one that will never be surpassed. As Ralph Kiner, who shared broadcasting duties for the Mets that day in 1963, so aptly put it in an interview with this writer shortly before he died, "Sometime, somebody will do the same thing, I think, but it would be one of the most difficult records to break." In a sport where pitched perfect games are rare, and where three-hit perfect games such as Paciorek's are rarer still, the world of baseball may never again see the likes of the man whose brilliance at the plate and in the field that day set the standard for one-game careers, a standard that cannot be chased with intent but that must be equaled or exceeded inadvertently, almost accidentally.

"It certainly makes sense that someone would look at what I did as a great accomplishment, at least in the big picture," Paciorek said. "I was blessed to have been given that special moment to play and to have done as well as I did."

In the history of major-league baseball, out of thousands of pitchers, only twenty-three players have thrown perfect games. Many of those who accomplished the feat were proven pitchers of distinction who achieved long and successful careers—stars, Hall of Famers, legends. In the world of position players, in more than a century and encompassing hundreds of thousands of games, only one man has accomplished what Paciorek did: three hits in three at-bats during his only major-league appearance. If baseball continues to entertain fans for another hundred years, perhaps even longer, Paciorek, with his awe-inspiring thesaurus of base hits, RBI, runs scored, times reached on base, on-base percentage, and fielding percentage, will likely still stand alone at the top. His was, truly, a perfect game.

1

The Natural

The good hitter effectively hits the ball with authority at least 2.72 times out of 10 at bats.
— *John Paciorek,* The Principle of Baseball: And All There Is to Know About Hitting

To those who knew him John Paciorek was a natural. Considering his youth, inexperience, and the chronic back pain caused by a congenital condition that was exacerbated by torn muscles, as a niche athlete he may have been the greatest major-league baseball player of all time. He certainly wasn't the greatest player over an extended period, but he is and likely will remain the greatest one-game—and only one game—position player in baseball history. The date? September 29, 1963. On that day, during the only game of his major-league baseball "career," Paciorek exceeded his own barometer for success—2.72 hits every 10 at-bats—to produce the greatest result for any individual who never again would play in the major leagues. The unique accomplishment also made him one of the most intriguing baseball figures of all time—an Eddie Gaedel with height, to revive the St. Louis Browns' now-infamous forty-three-inch midget, who wore uniform number 1/8 and whom owner Bill Veeck signed in 1951 for the sole purpose of drawing a walk. Taking into account Paciorek's age (he was still a teenager), his batting average (he had hit just over .200 when he was assigned to play for the big club), his dearth of professional baseball experience (he had played just one season of single-A ball), and the chronic back injury (it hurt him almost every day) that almost kept him out of the lineup that fall day when the Houston Colt .45s nearly-all-rookie starting lineup crushed the New York Mets, 13–4, what Paciorek accomplished speaks for itself. It is something no one else has since replicated or surpassed. Nor has anyone come close to replicating or surpassing it, nor is anyone likely to. Why? Because nowadays it is virtually un-heard of for any prospect playing for a sophisticated organization to receive a major-league assignment so lightly, on the whim of man-agement or with little likelihood that the player will stay with the team for at least a week or two and eventually become a useful con-tributor to its long-term success. At the same time, to beat Paciorek a player would have to go 4 for 4 and never play again—an unlikely prospect. What Paciorek accomplished is greatness in its purest form, not the caliber of greatness that makes for long and statistically im-pressive careers but the *grande capacité* that transcends long and im-pressive careers to become the majesty of brief careers that grow more legendary—larger—with each passing year. For Paciorek, his was a career that both *was* and *might have been*, one that started with a vengeance, lasted but a moment in time—a cup of coffee, as the ballplayers like to say—and that through the years has grown to leg-endary status, a monument of athleticism that people still talk about from Fenway Park to Dodger Stadium, where the Los Angeles Dodgers—his brother Tom's team for six seasons—began playing when Paciorek was merely a great high school athlete.

"It was like a dream—I couldn't believe it was happening," Paciorek said of his major-league debut. "I don't know why, but everything seemed to slow down when I faced major league pitching."[6]

Despite his accomplishment, not everyone remembers Paciorek—he even escapes the recollection of some who were at the ball game that day. Folks like broadcasting legend Gene Elston. Reached by telephone at his Houston, Texas, home, Elston, the iconoclastic play-by-play announcer for the Colt .45s and later the Houston Astros, could not recall either Paciorek or his performance—even after some prodding.

"I don't remember," said Elston, whose advancing years—he was ninety-one at the time—might have contributed to his amnesia. They probably did. In 2008, just five years earlier, Elston had penned a *Gene Elston's Journal* column for the Houston Astros titled "One-Game Gamers" in which he espoused Paciorek in the same breath as the diminutive Gaedel, Veeck's theoretical secret weapon who became a major-league dud. Gaedel's charge on that historic day? Not to swing: "If you so much as swing that bat at the plate I'll kill you," warned Veeck, who died in 1986. "No—I won't," he corrected himself, "but I can get the job done cut rate"—a reference to Gaedel's cut-rate size.[7]

Wrote Elston:

> While John's big league career lasted only one game, younger brother Tom Paciorek enjoyed an 18-year career in the majors, playing for the Dodgers, Braves, Mariners, White Sox, Mets and Rangers from 1970 to 1987. Baby brother Jim Paciorek had a 48-game major league career with the Brewers in 1987, batting .228.

But at family gatherings John can still brag that he had a higher career batting average than his siblings: a 1.000 mark that can never be topped.

Third baseman Bob Aspromonte, who collected two hits in Paciorek's debut game, had only a slightly better recollection of events than Elston.

"I can't put the pieces together, because it was fifty years ago, but I remember there was something unusual about [his] situation," Aspromonte said of Paciorek. "I can't define it . . . detail-wise, not really."

That Paciorek is forgettable to baseball cognoscenti such as Elston and Aspromonte is understandable. Countless players have begun their careers with a spate of hits and continued playing for years, even decades, making them easier to recall as their names entered the lexicon. Elston would agree that it's difficult to remember everyone who rode through the Texas franchise in its early, more forgettable seasons and whose names he spoke through the microphone over many years, especially the more obscure ones. At game time Paciorek certainly was obscure. And while he performed well that day, to many he remains obscure, albeit an obscure legend.

As a major leaguer Bobby Bonds broke in with a spirited performance, hitting a grand slam in his first major-league at-bat—his only hit of the game—and continuing on to enjoy a substantial career. What Paciorek did on September 29, 1963, neither Bobby (who went 1 for 3 that day) nor his son Barry (1 for 1 in his debut), who ended his career as the major league's home run king, achieved: three hits and four runs scored (Bobby Bonds had four RBI to Paciorek's three) in his first major-league game. Neither did Stan Musial (2 for 4), the onetime National League hits leader who made the All-Star team twenty-four times. Nor Hank Aaron (0 for 5), who on April 8, 1974, broke Babe Ruth's career mark of 714 home runs and who holds the major-league RBI record with 2,297. All four ballplayers had outstanding careers, yet what Paciorek accomplished in his single historic game also was outstanding, although in a much different way. He had, literally, a career game, posting one fewer hit than Bobby and Barry Bonds, Musial, and Aaron combined in their major-league debuts. His was a performance that prompted the *Houston Post* to confer on Paciorek the unofficial batting title for 1963. (The official champion that season was Tommy Davis of the Los Angeles Dodgers, who hit .326—a mere .674 less than Paciorek!)

Paciorek, who was born and reared in one of the greatest of all baseball cities—Detroit, Michigan—entered his only big league game at the age of 18 years, seven months, and eighteen days with no major-league experience and a history of pain resulting from his injured back. The back was almost too sore for him to play that afternoon eight weeks before President John F. Kennedy was assassinated. However, with less than a season of Class C ball (equivalent to today's Class A rookie ball) behind him he decided to give it a try even though he was barely out of high school. After all, this was the major leagues, the Big Show, an opportunity every minor-league ballplayer aspires to, and here it was being handed to him on a silver platter. It wasn't as if he had earned the chance to play that day, not really. It was simply an opportunity that was being dumped in his lap for one simple reason: to see what he would do. Paciorek would rise above the hesitation that hung in his brain due to the injury, play through the throbbing pain, give the final contest of the team's forgettable 1963 season his best effort, respond brilliantly to every chance he had both at the plate and in the outfield, and physically recover as well as he could during the long off season, he reckoned. After a period of extended R&R, some self-imposed exercise, and a few months of conditioning, he would be back in uniform the next season, ready to resume his promising major-league career, one that he hoped and believed would extend well beyond 1964—much the way his brother Tom would go on to enjoy a nearly two-decade career that began in 1970, the season after John at long last had retired.

It didn't quite work out that way.

Paciorek made the most of his time in the spotlight, adding perfect 1.000 slugging, on-base, and fielding percentages to his impressive hit, run, and RBI totals. His feat of reaching base that day five consecutive times is believed to be the most for any player at the start of a career. It was, clearly and in every respect, a perfect game. And if any one player seemed destined for greatness after just a single game in the major leagues it was Paciorek, the Catholic kid from St. Ladislaus High School in Hamtramck, Michigan, now and forever known affectionately as Mr. Perfection.

In the statistic-rich annals of major-league baseball, dating back to May 4, 1871, when the Fort Wayne Kekiongas beat the Cleveland Forest Cities, 2–0,[8] Paciorek's performance marked the single greatest one-game career in baseball history—one nearly matched by the great Aubrey "Yo-Yo" Epps.

Yo-Yo?

Epps, who died in 1984, was a catcher for the Pittsburgh Pirates who also made his major-league debut on September 29, although twenty-eight years earlier, on the final day of the 1935 season. Like Paciorek, Epps smacked three base hits, one of them a signature triple—unusual for a catcher—and finished with three RBI. But when the sun went down and Epps walked back to the clubhouse that day, his career had ended after one game, unbeknownst to him at the time. His batting average? A cool .750. Unlike Paciorek, in one of his official major-league at-bats Epps had gone hitless. Paciorek one-upped him to snag the unlikely designation as the greatest one-day wonder of all time, as the *Guinness Book of World Records* dubbed him in its 1990 edition. More than half a century later it is virtually certain the mark will never be eclipsed.

Still, Epps held the title of greatest one-game phenom for nearly three decades. Several years before his death he discussed his ephemeral career in a telephone interview with this writer: Following the game, "I came down with pneumonia," he said matter-of-factly, adding that he never was able to return to the major-league roster. Despite every effort to pull himself back up, Epps spent the rest of his career languishing in the minor leagues before disappearing into the humdrum world of conventional employment.

Certainly, Paciorek, like Epps, is a footnote in baseball lore, or maybe an asterisk. His career began after lunch and ended before supper. It was finished before he had time to rise from the bench and walk from the team's dugout to his locker. Before most of the sparse "crowd" of 3,899 fans in attendance that day had time to walk from their seats to their cars, Paciorek was through. Finis. His career, which had started with such promise, lasted just 148 minutes. A mere eight thousand seconds. Then, he was done—gone from major-league baseball forever, although destined to attain status as a baseball legend, a player who becomes better known with each passing year. John Paciorek was gone, but forgotten only temporarily.

Paciorek had no idea what was in store for him on the day he took the field. The muscular right fielder, who was named Associated Press "Player of the Day" after the game, had every expectation of ascending to baseball stardom, much like the revered Musial, who at the same time just 840 miles from Houston's Colt Stadium was playing in his final major-league game. Musial's career, which spanned twenty-two seasons, was the stuff that legends are made of; so, too, was Paciorek's, which spanned just over two hours and twenty minutes. During the afternoon he would receive twenty-three pitches from three different hurlers: Larry Bearnarth, Ed Bauta and Grover Powell. Of those pitches, thirteen were balls, four were strikes (two of them called), three were fouled off, and three were hit for singles. If there was anything imperfect about Paciorek's debut it was the two swinging and two called strikes he was charged with, the three balls that were fouled off, and the one time he failed to score: after Paciorek singled in the eighth inning, pinch hitter Dave Adlesh, who also was a rookie, hit back to the box and into a double play, sending both players to the dugout. Following a spectacular day at the plate Paciorek would never again run the base paths in a big-league game.

Playing elsewhere that day was Ken Hubbs, a smooth-fielding second baseman who also was competing in his final major-league game. Hubbs, Rookie of the Year the previous season and a Gold Glove winner as a budding star for the Chicago Cubs, would die in an airplane crash less than five months after the 1963 season ended. In his final game with the Cubs the twenty-one-year-old Hubbs, who had debuted at the age of nineteen to vast acclaim, went 0 for 3 to finish his second full season in the majors with eight home runs, forty-eight RBI, and a .modest 237 batting average. Unlike Musial, with two hits, and Paciorek, with three, Hubbs would leave baseball with goose eggs in the box score.

A fourth player ending his career that day was a pitcher, popular

Jim Umbricht, Paciorek's teammate and the winning pitcher in that final game of the 1963 season. Umbricht would die of cancer just seven weeks after Hubbs, on April 8, 1964, prompting the team to retire his jersey—a first for the Houston organization and, some argue, an honor based more on emotion than athleticism. Umbricht was a fine pitcher, but the retirement of his jersey speaks more about his character than his repertoire of pitches.

Musial, Hubbs, Paciorek, Umbricht: one player ordained for the Hall of Fame, retiring by choice; another on the cusp of greatness, retired tragically by the crash of a plane he was piloting; the third only a raw rookie with loads of talent, retired by injury; and a journeyman pitcher beloved by teammates and fans alike, retired by cancer. Each was significant in his own way, each playing in his final major-league game on the same day, all remembered for distinctly different careers, skill sets, and personalities. Two of them wouldn't live out the year, dying within weeks of each other, one would live for another half century, and the fourth—Paciorek, who is happy, healthy, and thriving—had high hopes of continuing his hot streak six months down the road when a new season, a season of hope and promise, would begin. Some wondered, perhaps in jest, whether any pitcher could ever get him out.

For Paciorek, there would be no next season, at least not at the major-league level—his career would resume in the minor leagues, with teams like the Durham Bulls, Reno Silver Sox, and, finally, the double-A Waterbury Indians. There would be no big salary, no fan club, no adoring groupies—"baseball Annies,"[9] they were called—following him to the team motor hotel after games, no fast women pleading for his attention at every turn or turnstile. Instead, he would struggle in the minor leagues for six more seasons before finally giving up on his dream of returning to the major leagues. If ever the term *one-game wonder* was an apt tag for a baseball player, it was certainly that in describing Paciorek, whose departure from baseball was a major-league disappointment. He rose fast, fell hard, and drifted into retirement so inauspiciously that by the time he exited baseball hardly anyone—perhaps only his family, close friends, and a few teammates—noticed he was no longer playing. Still, Paciorek was a one-game wonder, a man who on one glorious autumn afternoon in sweltering Houston weather put together his own version of perfection.

"I always wanted to be the best I could be," Paciorek said.[10] On that day, he *was* the best. He was absolutely perfect.

Hamtramck

Only two cities have ever won both the Little League and
Pony League World Series . . . Hamtramck is [one].
—*Ted Kulfan,* Detroit News

On a road map of Michigan with the Greater Detroit area shaded, the town of Hamtramck (pronounced *ham-TRAM-ick*) appears like a speck of soot on a child's drawing of home plate. It is surrounded by other specks, places like Bell Isle Park and Windsor and Ferndale. Even Hamtramck's website makes the city sound like a stepchild of sorts: "Hamtramck is mostly surrounded by Detroit, except [for] a small common border with the city of Highland Park."[11]

Situated in southeast Michigan and encompassing just two square miles, Hamtramck was named for Colonel Jean Francois Hamtramck, a Revolutionary War figure who occupied Detroit after British troops who remained in the country following the conflict were forced to abandon all forts still under their control in 1796. While less prominent than other Revolutionary War officers, Hamtramck did serve his country and what is now Michigan, in particular the area that would become Hamtramck, with distinction. A member of the famed Continental army, he twice received commendations for bravery from General George Washington, although his service record does list a demotion early in his career before he ascended to the rank of colonel. Hamtramck's name was permanently etched in the annals of Michigan history when Washington sent founding father John Jay across the pond to secure a treaty that would unequivocally identify the US borders. The treaty called for the British to depart from all forts they occupied within the existing boundaries of the United States; Colonel Hamtramck was ordered to receive Detroit. In 1798 much of Michigan, Wisconsin, and Ohio was assembled into one county, which in turn was divided into four townships: Detroit, Sergeant, Mackinaw, and Hamtramck.

Today Hamtramck is an independent municipality of twenty-three thousand people lying just south of Grosse Pointe Woods and west of Grosse Pointe Park. It is also five miles from the center of Detroit, where on February 11, 1945, John Francis Paciorek was born to John Joseph Paciorek and Frances Ann (Loszewski) Paciorek at St. Joseph Mercy Hospital. His birth came forty-four years after the heavily Polish community was established as a village, a settlement where the Paciorek brothers—there were five in all, and three sisters—would spend much of their time growing up, playing baseball on fields that to them must have seemed like Tiger Stadium itself. In the Paciorek family, sports had been a priority *ab ovo*—from day one.

Both Detroit and Hamtramck were perfect environments for a boy who hoped to become a major-league baseball player. Detroit proper is home to the Tigers, winners of four World Series,[12] and the Motor City has produced numerous high-profile major-league

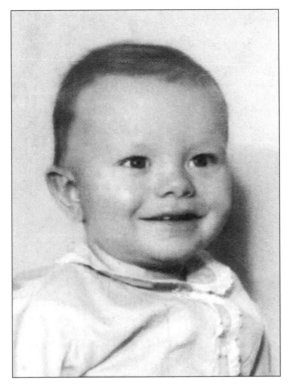

Early photo of Paciorek, age 1.

ballplayers. A sampling includes Hall of Famer Hal Newhouser, a four-time Most Valuable Player for the Tigers and a pitcher who led the American League in victories four times; Frank Tanana, who won 240 games and struck out 2,773 batters in twenty-one major-league seasons—eight of them with his hometown Tigers; Bob Welch, the 1990 Cy Young Award winner and a two-time All-Star who won 211 games for the Los Angeles Dodgers and Oakland Athletics; and Milt Pappas, also a two-time All-Star who won 209 games in seventeen seasons with four different teams.

Like Detroit, Hamtramck developed a reputation as a breeding ground for young ballplayers, and during the 1940s and 1950s grooming often began early in a boy's life. For young John, baseball and football competed for attention as far back as he can remember, and those sports, along with basketball, remained compelling interests through his graduation from high school.

The Pacioreks lived on Moenart Street, a quiet avenue situated in a blue-collar Catholic neighborhood not far from Six Mile Road. Because the houses on Moenart Street were built close together, separated by only narrow walkways, the family's two-story home and others on the block appeared larger than they actually were to those walking along the tree-lined street. However, the eight children and their parents were squeezed tightly into three small bedrooms, sometimes sleeping three to a bed. After bills were paid and food was put on the table there was little money left over for fun and entertainment, and the family even received welfare assistance for a short time. With so many children it is difficult to determine whether the

Brother Bobby poses in front of the time-worn family home at 13432 Moenart St., Detroit, in 2013.

Taking Holy Communion, age 9, c.1954

Paciorek family truly was poor, as Tom has stated, or simply poor relative to the large number of children who needed to be fed and clothed. Tom noted that the family was the last in the neighborhood to purchase a television set.[13] Perhaps they truly were poor.

What the family lacked financially the parents made up for spiritually, enrolling the eldest children at Transfiguration School and later St. Ladislaus High School when they were old enough to attend. It was at St. Ladislaus where John began to excel in sports beyond

With teammate Chet Jarema receiving Michigan High School Athletic
Association plaque as District 8 Class B champions in football from
unidentified St. Ladislaus High School clergyman, c. 1961

the level of skill that most of his friends were demonstrating. While
attending St. Ladislaus something more ominous also began to occur,
something that engulfed not only John but brothers Tom and Bobby,
too. Decades later that "something" would make headlines.

Despite their financial hardships Paciorek's father was a dedicated
and tireless automobile assembly-line employee who spent forty
years working for Chrysler-Plymouth. Although he rose early to
begin work and returned home from the plant dead tired, he always
had enough energy left to toss a baseball around with the boys in
the front yard before dinner.

To test-drive the catching and throwing skills taught to him by
his muscular father, a formidable baseball player in his own right

who was pursued by scouts only to have his own parents chase them off with a broomstick, Paciorek and his friends would walk five blocks to Lasky Park or sprawling Jayne Field near the Detroit Public Library for a game of pickup baseball or tackle football. "There was so much grass there that we made our own baseball diamonds," he said. "We played a lot of baseball and a lot of football. Lasky also had a pond that froze over in the winter, and we played hockey there or swam in it during the summer."

Paciorek also credits his daily six-block jaunts—actually, runs—to and from Transfiguration School with more than preparing him for high school football. He began the regimen in kindergarten and continued it through his early years in grade school.

"It's funny how you develop your skills," he said. "I would run those six blocks to school heading directly at trees and cars, cutting and spinning at the last second to avoid hitting them. Every once in a while I would smash into a parked car or tree. Later on, when I played high school football, I was really elusive and could fake out people on the opposing team because I had practiced running at trees and cars and making quick moves. It became instinctive."

Although loved by his father, Paciorek recalls him as a tough taskmaster who believed in using the rod rather than risk spoiling the child. It was that attitude that embedded in Paciorek a distain for his studies that ultimately led him to sign a baseball contract after his senior year at St. Ladislaus, a parochial school where Catholicism and sports went hand in hand.

"School and I were not good together, I had a horrible educational experience all of my life," he said. "It stemmed from the fact that my dad had not finished high school and he knew the importance of an education. The effort he put in to try and help us in

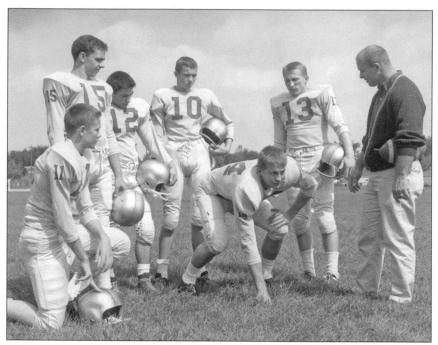

Demonstrating a three-point stance as coach and teammates
at St. Ladislaus High School look on approvingly, c. 1961

every aspect of our education was admirable, but if I didn't read the right word he would hit me in the back of the head. It got to the point where I couldn't see the next page, I was just waiting for the next hit to come.

"I was going to attend the University of Houston [on a football scholarship], and I was so grateful that I signed a pro baseball contract instead because I didn't want to go to college."

As a result of his father's aggressive tutelage, Paciorek's studies always took a back seat to sports, and he, like his brothers, used every opportunity to practice. When friends weren't around to play with the brothers they would toss a tennis ball hard against the front steps of their home, often fielding it after an unpredictable bounce to further hone their skills. Paciorek fielded those balls using his "prized

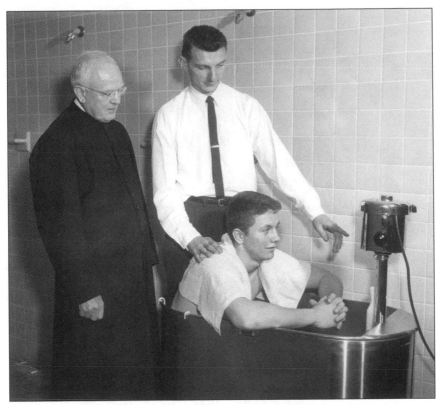

Receiving whirlpool treatment as high school coach John
Radwanski and an unidentified clergyman look on, c. 1961

possession": a glove purchased for him by his uncle.

"Our front porch steps were blasted to shreds by the constant battering of tennis balls," he said. "That's how we learned to throw and catch, using our backhand and forehand depending upon which direction the ball bounced."

Paciorek attended school in Hamtramck not only with his brother Tom, but also with Little League legend Art "Pinky" Deras, who perfected his own baseball skills as a Pony League teammate of Tom, also was a fixture on the ball fields at Hamtramck.

It was Pinky Deras, nicknamed by his grandmother for reasons he was never told, who in 1959 enjoyed the finest Little League season of anyone, leading Hamtramck to the Little League World Series title. During that season the 135-pound Deras threw eighteen complete games, won eighteen times, recorded sixteen shutouts, threw ten no-hitters, and struck out 298 batters. He also hit thirty-three home runs—thirteen of them in the thirteen tournament games his team won—batting an astounding .641 and driving in 112 runs. In the final game of the Little League World Series, Deras led his team to a 12–0 victory over West Auburn, California, running his streak of consecutive scoreless innings pitched to seventy-five—in Little League numbers that translates to twelve consecutive shutouts.[14] His statistics that season as both a hitter and a pitcher are still considered remarkable, and Deras was eventually featured in an Emmy-nominated documentary titled *The Legend of Pinky Deras: The Greatest Little Leaguer There Ever Was.*

"He was the best ever," said Tom Paciorek, a teammate of Deras on the Hamtramck Pony League world championship team. "Hitting off Pinky Deras was like hitting off Nolan Ryan from forty-five feet away. And if you pitched to him he hit a home run. He was unbelievable. Pinky never played a game in the big leagues, John played one game, and I played for eighteen years. I'll never understand it."

John shared his brother's assessment of their chum. "Pinky Deras was something else. He holds all the Little League records."

John Paciorek, too, was something else. Deras, who played against him only once, shortly before Deras retired from professional baseball after the 1968 season, said Paciorek "was probably the best all-around high school athlete to come out of Michigan. Football, baseball, and basketball—he was all-state in all three." When asked about the perfect game, Deras was emphatic: "Three for three answers the question—he was perfect. Too bad he had the injury, because who knows what would have happened after that. The only player I would compare him with would be Tony Conigliaro—I think they were similar-type players."

In 1961, two years after the Little League world championship, Deras and Tom Paciorek would lead Hamtramck to the Pony League world title—the first time that one community had won both the Little League and Pony League world championships, a feat they nearly accomplished in consecutive years. Thanks to two up-and-coming young ballplayers, and a third who would make a splash later as a member of the Houston Colt .45s, the city of Hamtramck was on the sporting map to stay.

As boys, Deras's and Tom Paciorek's acumen on the field did not go unnoticed; nor did the potential that John was beginning to show. Unlike Deras, he played Little League ball for only two years and was by his own admission "a horrible hitter . . . I was definitely afraid of the ball," although while playing for the Hamtramck Little League Cardinals he learned for the first time to throw his weight into a pitch rather than step away as it sped toward home plate. Just seven years after that epiphany—one that christened him a power hitter—and only a few short seasons after playing Pony League and American Legion ball, John Paciorek would find himself in the major leagues.

At that moment of realization any doubt that a career in sports awaited Paciorek was dissolved. However, which sport he would pursue still remained the big question; he later earned high school all-America honors in football and all-state honors in football, baseball, and basketball.

"I thought I was going to become a baseball player in baseball season and a football player in football season, and in between I'd

Taking a swing during an American Legion game, c. 1962

do a little boxing," he said. "I could kick a football seventy yards and at one point I even contemplated becoming a professional kicker."

John's proclivity for baseball and his ability to play the game at a high level were becoming known around Detroit. When he was barely into his teens a number of the area's top ballplayers were invited to play in a showcase event at Tiger Stadium, and he was selected for the team. Joining him was future Tiger Willie Horton. Paciorek hit two doubles that day, to either side of dead center field. The sound of the ball popping off the bat left him spellbound with excitement. "It sounded like it exploded off the bat," he said, and the power he was able to unleash seemed to mesmerize him. He liked the feeling that blasting a baseball gave him.

Paciorek continued to improve, and when he entered high school in 1958 it was a foregone conclusion that he would make the varsity baseball team as a freshman. Unfortunately, he weighed only 119 pounds, and the deficit in bulk concerned him. So much that he began to lift weights, people—anything he could find—while eating

Getting a shot off despite defenders during
St. Ladislaus High School game, c. 1961

as much as he could. As his weight lifting continued, so began a regimen that would lead to a series of injuries that would drive him out
of baseball.

By his senior year Paciorek's weight had nearly doubled to two
hundred pounds, and at six foot two he had grown into a formida-

Kneeling with the cast from a high school play, c. 1962.

ble-looking athlete. A talented one, too, excelling at every sport he played. By his final year in high school, scholarship offers were beginning to come in. In addition to the University of Houston, the more prominent schools interested in his quarterback/running back talents included two perennial powerhouses: the University of Alabama and the University of Michigan. However, Paciorek, still a disinterested student, along with brother Tom and friend Deras, had other dreams.

"It didn't impress me," Paciorek said of the recruiting he experienced from big-time colleges, "because I didn't want any part of an education."

Within a couple years of the Pony League championship the Paciorek brothers and Deras all found themselves fulfilling their dreams of playing professional baseball, although for Deras his earlier accomplishments as a Little League, Pony League, and high school star would have to suffice. He spent five seasons in the St. Louis Cardinals organization, eventually earning a promotion to double-A ball, while brothers John and Tom rose to the major-league level. Younger brother Jim, who also played briefly in the major leagues, was born in 1960—the year between the Little League and Pony League championships—and was not old enough to play competitively with either Deras, whose professional baseball career ironically ended at Modesto, where Paciorek's had begun, or with brothers Tom and John.

"I was too young, he left at seventeen," Jim said of brother John. "From what I've heard he was pretty special. He had good size and speed and people said he might have been the next Mickey Mantle. It's just a shame that he did get hurt and never made it back [to the major leagues]."

While most of the eight Paciorek children eventually developed a love for sports, and three of them became major-league ballplayers, it was John who first rose to prominence as a big leaguer, someone who could hit the ball a country mile.

"He was bigger and faster and stronger than anyone else," Tom Paciorek said.

John likely inherited that power, which as a player allowed him to hit vertiginous home runs, from his father.

"My dad used to say that as kids we all needed stronger wrists and hands and that the best way to build up our strength was to wash floors and scrub dishes," he said.

In the Paciorek household there were always plenty of dishes to wash and floors to scrub, and many pairs of strong hands and wrists to wash them. In addition to onetime big leaguers John, Tom, and Jim, there were Michael, who played minor-league baseball from 1973 to 1977, Bobby, Marilyn, Joanne, and Carol. Aside from the endless hours spent washing dishes, only one thing might have stood in the way of the brothers' success: the Reverend Gerald Shirilla.

In a highly publicized revelation of abuse, John said Shirilla, who taught religion at St. Ladislaus and had gained the confidence of the brothers' parents, began helping him work on term papers and fill out college applications during his senior year in high school. He was known to the elder Pacioreks and they didn't question his motives. Perhaps they should have. According to Paciorek, at some point in 1961, in the family's backyard, the future priest made an unwanted sexual advance toward the sixteen-year-old youth. Paciorek, who was caught off guard, managed to convince the man to stop, but he only ceased with him. In 1962 the priest reportedly turned his attention to Tom, beginning a succession of molestations that continued for several years. "I was molested by him for a period of four years," Tom said. "I would refer to them as attacks. I would say there was at least a hundred of them."[15] Tom says the abuse, which often occurred during the evenings when Shirilla took him to Sacred Heart Academy, where his studies for the priesthood were ongoing, continued until he graduated from St. Ladislaus High and enrolled at the University of Houston.

Brothers Michael and Bobby also say they were victims of the priest, although Jim was not. It was Michael who first revealed that he had been molested as a pre-adolescent during conversations he had with his brothers in the 1980s. Bobby said his abuse at the hands of Shirilla began in junior high school.[16]

Shirilla, who denied the allegations, was never charged with a crime after the brothers went public with their claims beginning in 2002, largely because the statute of limitations had expired. However, while working as a parish priest in Alpena, Michigan, Shirilla was removed shortly before Tom Paciorek went public about the molestation in 2002.[17] Since the Paciorek revelations the brothers have gamely continued on with their lives. Shirilla died in 2004.

Lou DeNunzio, the local scout who selected Paciorek to play in the Tiger Stadium exhibition, was among the first to get it right. He could see that Paciorek was a legitimate prospect and early on gave him exposure as well as experience playing before crowds. After DeNunzio, others also would get it right. The next to come along was Paul Richards, the Colts' general manager. After the team wrapped up its first season in September 1962 Richards, a former catcher, traveled to Michigan in the hope of convincing Paciorek to sign a contract with the up-and-coming expansion team, which would begin its second season of play the following year.

"Paul Richards watched me play at St. Ladislaus High, and one day he stopped by the house for a visit," Paciorek said. "I told him I was thinking about attending college and he promised to offer me enough money that I wouldn't have to go to college. At that point I was six two and weighed more than two hundred pounds and I ran pretty well. Most important, I was a good all-around ballplayer. In my youthful mind I believed Mr. Richards was going to make me a millionaire."

Looking on (far right) with coach and teammates during an
instructional session at St. Ladislaus High School, 1962.

The year was 1962 and Paciorek, who at seventeen was barely
old enough to shave, was unaccustomed to the finer things in life as
he pondered the major-league contract that Richards was likely to
offer him. Among those finer things were fine restaurants and fine
steaks. Knowing young men and how they like to eat, Richards,
whose middle name was Rapier—defined as a slender, sharply
pointed sword—and assistant general manager Eddie Robinson decided to play the restaurant card with Paciorek and his parents, who
brought along Tom and toddler Jim. A shrewd baseball man, he
probably figured he could smooth the way toward signing the boy

Conferring with his catcher during a
St. Ladislaus High School game, c. 1962.

for a reasonable bonus simply by plying him with—what else?—
beef, along with all the trimmings.

"We had never been to a restaurant before," recalled Tom. "We
had steaks and spaghetti and ate like horses. Finally, Mr. Richards
said, 'Hey, you want anything else—dessert or anything?' John said,
'Yeah, I'd like to have another one of those steaks.' I think they

looked at the bill and left with tears in their eyes."

The story is reminiscent of a young Ted Williams, who at age twenty was two years older than Paciorek when he was called up to the major leagues. During his first season in the minors, playing for the San Diego Padres of the Pacific Coast League, Williams, too, developed a reputation for eating voraciously. "He'd put away two T-bone steaks and a platter of rolls for breakfast," teammate George Myatt recalled.[18]

Whether it was the steaks or the opportunity to dine out with the general manager of a major-league ball club, or simply the fact that the Colts wanted him badly enough to buy him dinner, it worked: Paciorek signed a contract with Houston on August 15, 1962. He said his mind had been made up before even meeting Richards for dinner, although Richards did not know that. "I definitely wanted to sign a contract, there was nothing that could have stopped that. There is no doubt that I wanted a taste of everything the Colts might want to offer me"—including a free meal.

"Had I not suffered a sprained ankle playing basketball I clearly would have been in a better place to bargain. As a result, the scouts that Mr. Richards sent to watch me play never saw me at my best. That kept my bargaining power down."

The amount of bonus money Paciorek received is somewhat in dispute, although not in Paciorek's mind. How much did Richards offer? Far less than the $80,000 that Little League whiz kid Deras received for signing with the Cardinals. "The press reported that I was offered $90,000, but that wasn't correct. It was probably half that. I received $15,000, my parents received $15,000, and I received another $15,000 my first year with the organization along with my $500-per-month regular salary. Because of my bad ankle it

In Houston Colt .45s uniform, 1962
(Photo courtesy of the Houston Astros)

wasn't easy getting *that*."

Paciorek then explained, "I was young and perhaps thought more highly of myself than I should have. I felt I deserved the same bonus that all of the high-priced young ballplayers were receiving. I believed $100,000 was reasonable."

Even so, $45,000 was a huge amount of money for a teenager, a lad who had grown up lacking the things that only a good education and the income it promised could ultimately provide. According to Paciorek, who two years hence would use some of that bonus money to buy himself a brand-new Chevrolet Malibu convertible, his father understood the importance of higher education and wisely insisted that the Colts include a scholarship fund that eventually would pay for his son to attend college if he wished to after his playing days—or playing day, as it turned out—were over. His contract at last signed, Paciorek hit the road in October 1962 for a town he had never been to and possibly never even heard of: Apache Junction, where the Colts assigned him to play in the Arizona Instructional League. With money in hand, the wind at his back, and a budding major-league career within grasp, at least on paper Paciorek was a professional baseball player due all the respect—and eventual acrimony—that the title conferred. The world was his oyster.

In light of Richards's hard bargaining the Colts, too, were pleased to at last get Paciorek's signature down on paper. After signing the young man, the former major-league player and manager described his protégé as someone who had the potential to grow into one of the best hitters for power and most versatile players in the major leagues. The confident Paciorek did not dispute Richards's unwavering belief in him. Instead, he reported to the Arizona Instructional League ready to stamp an exclamation mark on it.

"I did very well there," Paciorek said. "Al Kaline had played for the Tigers when he was eighteen and I definitely thought I could play in the majors at eighteen. I was a solid hitter and I wasn't a bit anxious. I believed in my heart that I belonged on a major-league team."

Danny Coombs, a teammate of Paciorek in the Instructional League and at Modesto and Houston, describes himself as a "fringe major leaguer." The nine-year veteran, who also played with the San Diego Padres, remembers Paciorek as someone who had all the tools necessary to be a star player.

"Oh, yes, he was a big bonus baby from Michigan," he said. "He wore ankle weights. They brought him to the big leagues and I think he injured his back. That was the end of his career . . . I knew he had a great day.

"He was a character," added Coombs, who until contacted thought Paciorek had gone 4 for 4 in his debut. "He had a lot of athletic ability, he was really talented . . . he had a great arm on him, he ran well, he was a good-sized kid, had good power, strong as a bull."

From the Arizona Instructional League it was on to the Colts' 1963 spring training camp, also in Apache Junction, where Paciorek met his future major-league manager Harry Craft, whom he described as "a nice guy, calm" but someone whose hesitation to correct player mistakes in a timely fashion instilled in himself the imperative to immediately correct errors in the young athletes he now instructs. Although Paciorek played well the Colts assigned him to the team's training camp at Moultrie, Georgia, where he played respectably despite the poor facilities there.

"The field reminded me of a cow pasture," he said. "From my

vantage point in the outfield, where I stood in a gully, I couldn't see home plate. For a batter the visibility was terrible—there was no green backdrop, and as a result the ball blended in with the light background and made seeing difficult. Combine that with the fast and sometimes wild pitchers I was facing and I only wanted to get out of there alive."

The state of the ball field may have been reflected in Paciorek's attitude and ultimately in his play. As Houston waited patiently for his offensive clout to kick into high gear, it didn't. "I'm not sure why but I just wasn't motivated. I should have taken advantage of my good fortune as a professional ballplayer instead of acting like a teenager."

Still, he played reasonably well—he always played well. "I probably did fairly well, except I wasn't gutting it out because the hitters didn't have a green background in the outfield and I didn't want to get hurt. I don't think I did poorly, I can't remember ever doing poorly."

He still needed more experience, however, and the first thing Paciorek learned was that making a big-league roster was not going to be as easy as he thought, although ultimately it would be easier for him than it is for most players. There would be disappointments along the way, and his first one came when the Colts sent him down to play Class C ball at Modesto in the California League to gain some experience. Ironically, the move was made because Paciorek had played well in Arizona and Georgia—not because he hadn't played well enough. He started off the season strong, surprising no one.

"I didn't realize it, but Mr. Richards was on my side. He said he wanted me to play at a level where I could develop my skills—he didn't want me languishing on the Colt .45s' bench.

"I felt let down. For my eighteen-year-old mind the minor leagues was the worst place I could be."

Despite Richards's explanation Paciorek felt demoted—not only from a baseball perspective, but also emotionally. He felt let down by the team he had just skipped college for—over twin steaks, no less.

If the Colts and Richards were disappointed that he wasn't busting down fences in Arizona the front office didn't show it, assigning him to start in center field for Modesto on opening day. Raymond Staub, brother of Houston's Rusty Staub, remembers him all too well:

> I played center field at Modesto the year before John was there. I was [then] moved to another team [the Moultrie Colt .22s, a Class D affiliation in the Georgia–Florida League], led the league in hitting, and had a very good season. When I received my contract in early spring of the following year it had a 20 percent pay cut in it. I thought, *What? This is crazy!* So I wrote on the contract, "Please, send me *my* contract—this can't be mine," and I sent it back to Houston. They responded, "What are you, a smart aleck?" I said, "How can I lead a league in hitting and you give me a 20 percent cut?" They said, "Well, you don't hit the home runs."
>
> I had the good fortune to return to Modesto at the beginning of the 1963 season. My recollection is that Paciorek had signed a contract with Houston during the off season. It was a wonderful contract and he was very

much worth it. We went to Modesto together and . . . he played center field. He never did hit the amount of home runs that it was theoretically supposed to be, but he did hit home runs. And if he caught one real good, Yellowstone wasn't going to hold it.

On another occasion Staub's wife and her father drove out from New Orleans to watch a Modesto Colts game. Because his father-in-law had never seen Staub play professionally, and because the two were only going to be in town for one game, Staub asked manager Dave Philley if he could start in center field that day instead of Paciorek. Philley agreed. However, during warm-ups prior to the game a group of scouts from the parent club suddenly showed up unannounced.

"They were all coming to see somebody, and guess who it wasn't," he said. "It was me they were not coming to see—and I didn't play center field."

Instead, Paciorek started in center field as usual, and Staub was relegated to coaching first base. During the entire season Staub batted only three times, going 0 for 3. Seeing the writing on the wall, he left baseball for good after the season ended, although fifty years later he harbors no ill will toward the man who displaced him in the outfield—effectively ending his career. "He was a great prospect and deserved everything he got, I just wanted to be out there myself. He was a good guy."

Staub described Paciorek as a "gifted" ballplayer, someone who exceeded his brother in that respect. "I think he was more gifted [than Tom Paciorek]," he said. "A lot of people think his weight lifting probably deterred a lot of his effectiveness on the field."

Playing under Philley, an old-school manager whose toughness reflected the days when athletes played through their injuries, Paciorek hit .326 with two home runs and a team-leading twelve RBI during the first thirteen games at Modesto. At last he was motivated and hustling, running everywhere. He would race in from his outfield position in an effort to beat his teammates off the field. He would sprint in to beat his third baseman to the dugout. He would back up everyone. On more than one occasion he even made putouts at third base, catching balls that should have been caught by an infielder or by a left fielder playing shallow. "They thought I was a flake," Paciorek said, although, "Eventually, the people who knew me liked me. They came to realize that the hustle was good, that my intent wasn't to make anyone look bad. I couldn't stand to do anything half baked . . . I had inexhaustible energy."

He again began lifting weights, this time in combination with headstands, handstands, and neck rolls. "There was no rhyme nor reason for the exercises I was focusing on every day," he said. "Nothing at all. In addition to the countless push-ups and sit-ups I did I ran around wearing lead ankle weights, thinking that would increase my speed. Then, after all of the exercising, I'd go out and try to play baseball. It's no wonder I was hurting."

All the while Paciorek marched to the beat of a different drummer. When the team was assigned to run laps, he headed in the opposite direction of the other players so that no teammate could block his path and slow him down. In all things he wanted to finish first.

As the self-inflicted beating on his body continued, Paciorek began to experience upper-back problems that worsened as he continued playing. At one point his neck became so badly strained that he was unable to lift his throwing arm. The pain continued and his average dropped dramatically. Finally, he left the lineup and began sitting on the bench, where he started a new regimen of exercises in hopes of loosening his back, which had begun to stiffen due to lack of use. The irony was that Richards had sent Paciorek to a club that wouldn't have him languish on the bench because of his inexperience, and there he was in Modesto—languishing on the bench due to injury.

By September, Paciorek's average had dropped to .219. However, half of his sixty hits were for extra bases, and the big club could see that he had power. No one was discouraged, at least not overtly.

By August, when Modesto's season ended, Houston knew that its star of the future was having a difficult time just making it through the present. He was hurt, had been struggling at the plate, was frustrated at spending so much time on the bench, and probably wondered what the future really did hold for him. Then came the question.

In September 1963, several weeks after the California League play-offs had ended, Paciorek was summoned to Houston so that doctors could examine his sore back. While there, he received the surprise of his life when someone in the front office asked him if he might be fit enough to play in the last game of the season against the Mets.

"I was in a lot of pain, but my answer was: 'Yeah!' Nothing was going to keep me from playing in a major-league game."

In retrospect, the Colts' intent was clear: to showcase their cadre of promising young ballplayers, many of whom would go on to enjoy long and successful careers. The first opportunity occurred on September 27, 1963, when manager Craft started the all-rookie lineup, a collection of players who despite their youthful enthusiasm lost resoundingly to the lowly Mets, 10–3. Although Paciorek was in Houston to receive medical treatment at the time, he was not a part of that lineup. His opportunity would come two days later when Paciorek, a low minor leaguer who was injured, slumping, discouraged, and in Houston only to find out what was wrong with him, was catapulted into the starting lineup alongside players who would make up the heart of the team for the next ten years—including Rusty Staub, who played for the Colts and later the Houston Astros from 1963 through 1968. Staub and Paciorek were the two top baseball prospects in the country in 1962, according to Tom Paciorek. The offer to play came the day after the all-rookie squad lost to the Mets. According to John, the opportunity may have reflected the big club's belief that because he had been running and jumping and catching without apparent hindrance during recent practice sessions, he was fit enough to play in games.

"They just asked me, 'Would you like to play tomorrow?' I thought it was cool. There was no way I was going to miss that game. That caught me so off guard that I didn't have time to think. Heck yeah! If I'd have thought about it I'd have questioned whether I could do it because of my back.

"They never confided in me [why the Colts asked him to play]."

If the opportunity caught Paciorek off guard it didn't surprise Staub when his former roommate appeared in the starting lineup.

"He had so much talent," Staub said of Paciorek. "It's hard to believe he didn't succeed in baseball. No one was a better athlete than he was. He showed power . . . he was certainly a star in the making.

"Obviously, there was huge anticipation for what he might become."

Paciorek shared that anticipation. Despite his injuries, stiffness, and recent lack of playing time, the teen rookie was up to the challenge the Colts were presenting. After all, he had wanted to be a baseball player his entire life and here was a gift: an opportunity to play in the major leagues. Despite the pain, despite the possibility of exacerbating the injury, despite all of the things that were working against him, there was no way he would sit on the sidelines.

3

Play Ball

Records are made to be broken.
—Unknown

Mets announcer Lindsey Nelson: And the starting lineups for the game: For the Colt .45s Glenn Vaughan will lead off and play shortstop. Batting second, playing second base, Joe Morgan. Batting third in left field, Jim Wynn. The fourth batter will be the first baseman Rusty Staub. Batting fifth and playing third base, Bob Aspromonte. Batting sixth in center field, Ivan Murrell. Batting seventh, playing right field, John Paciorek . . .

With the baseball season winding down, Nelson's smooth-throated pronouncement of Houston's starting lineup was both the first public mention of Paciorek's name in the context of a major-league baseball game, and a dirge. On the one hand it must have sounded breathtaking to anyone who knew the teen and happened to be tuned in to the broadcast. Because the game was broadcast to New York and Houston, and because Paciorek was from Michigan, there probably were very few fans listening who actually knew him.

Nor did Paciorek recall alerting anyone to his good fortune before the game began—not even his family. On the other hand, Nelson's recitation marked the last time Paciorek would be publicly introduced before a big-league baseball game, though certainly no one knew it at the time.

Even though he was "pretty excited about playing in a major-league game," Paciorek said he held that excitement in check. "I can't recall that I called anybody to tell them I was going to be playing. I don't know whether my parents even knew afterward that I had played—I think I called them after the game from a hotel."

Why *would* he have told anyone? After all, the odds were against Paciorek accomplishing much of anything in his first major-league game. With his inexperience, prolonged injury, and the short notice that he would be playing at all, the deck was certainly stacked against him.

"Maybe my underlying feeling was, 'How could I expect to do anything in this game, what could I possibly do?' Then, one thing after another, the pieces fell together. Somebody was up there orchestrating things."

As Nelson finished introducing the players, Paciorek and his teammates trotted out onto the field and the four umpires moved into position to start the game.

"I loved the environment," Paciorek said. "I had been a big fish in a small pond, and I just knew I was going to be a big fish in a big pond."

Standing in right field as Colt .45s devotees trickled through the turnstiles was a good feeling for the energetic Paciorek, who was playing in a major-league ballpark for the third time in his life; his first appearance was during the exhibition at Tiger Stadium, and the second occurred his senior year in high school during the tryout for Richards at Wrigley Field in Chicago. Even though Colt Stadium was a temporary playing field designed to bridge completion of the Houston Astrodome, which was under construction on adjacent land, its grass was greener and more artistically mown, the infield dirt was finer and more expertly raked, and the pitching mound was exactly as it should have been, with the top of the rubber no more than ten inches higher than home plate. Even if the grass hadn't been greener and the dirt any finer than the playing surface at, say, John Thurman Field in Modesto, this relative baseball paradise would have seemed that way to Paciorek, who was playing before at least one legend that day: Mets manager Stengel. In sharp contrast with his first and only major-league game, Paciorek had no memory of his first minor-league game playing for Modesto.

Despite Nelson's broadcast of the starting lineup, despite Paciorek's proximity standing in the outfield, and despite his eagerness to bat for the first time, he was not yet a major-league ballplayer. That would occur momentarily, following the national anthem and Bearnarth's first pitch to rookie Ed Kranepool:

> **Nelson:** Hello everybody, Ed Kranepool is in, a left-hand batter. Chris Zachary into the windup, here's the first pitch of the game and it's in there for a called strike one.

Finally, there it was: With the first pitch the game was officially under way, and Paciorek's badge of honor had been bestowed, although certainly without fanfare. After eighteen years and countless hours spent at various playgrounds, ballparks, and neighborhoods in search of a school or cul-de-sac game, or simply seeking out friends with whom he could play a game of catch or over-the-line, Paciorek had made it. With pitcher Zachary's first thrust of a baseball sixty feet, six inches toward a piece of rubber shaped like a house, the Houston–Mets game was under way and Paciorek was officially a major-league ballplayer. His name would forever be etched in the ledgers of the sport as one of the comparatively few players going back more than a century who were gifted enough and blessed enough to make it to the major leagues. No matter what he did during the remainder of the game, or during any game or any season thereafter—if there were to be other games and other seasons—he would always be able to claim that he had reached the pinnacle of the sport he loved. With that one pitch to Kranepool, a called strike down the middle, right fielder Paciorek became a bona fide big-league ballplayer, just like Ruth, Aaron, Mantle, Honus Wagner, and the many other baseball greats and lesser-knowns who preceded him throughout the history of major-league baseball. Still a teenager, Paciorek's dream of becoming a big-league ballplayer had been realized in astoundingly quick fashion. As the future unfolded before him he was eagerly looking forward to many more compelling moments wearing a Houston Colt .45s uniform.

The first inning passed uneventfully, with the Mets going down quietly in the top half despite a hit batter and a walk; Houston closed out their half of the inning by going down in order. The Mets went down one–two–three in the top of the second, thanks in part to the efforts of Paciorek. He proved to be an able fielder, earning his first major-league putout at the expense of Mets left fielder Joe Hicks:

Nelson: Here's the 2–2 pitch, swung on [and] hit in the air to right field and John Paciorek is over and back and makes the catch, although he ran sort of a strange pattern getting over there.

Ralph Kiner: Looked like an end going after one of those passes.

Nelson: Wind is blowing rather stiffly out toward right, and that is why Paciorek faked a couple times in going over. That ball carried a little farther than he thought it was going to when it caught in that wind.

Paciorek repeated the effort two batters later with his second—and last—putout of the game, although the gusty wind was less of a factor with light-hitting shortstop Al Moran at bat and a 2–2 count:

Nelson: Here's the 2–2 pitch: hit in the air to the right side, and drifting back is Joe Morgan the second baseman. He's in short right field, it carries him on out and Paciorek calls him off and makes the catch. Morgan went out and called but the wind carried that ball on back so Paciorek called him off and made the catch.

In the bottom half of the second inning, after the rookie Staub grounded out to lead off and the veteran Aspromonte walked, Paciorek made his way nervously toward the batter's box for his first major-league at-bat. Just moments earlier he had watched from the on-deck circle as umpire Paul Pryor walked slowly toward a spot in front of home plate, then swung his six-foot-two, 220-pound frame

Posing in Colt .45s uniform, 1962
(Photo courtesy of the Houston Astros)

around to face the backstop. The routine that followed was one that Paciorek anticipated seeing thousands of times before his baseball career would end.

With his back to pitcher Bearnarth, a young right-hander who during the long 1963 season had won only three games while losing seven, Pryor pulled a small whisk broom from a well-hidden holster, bent down at the waist, and gave the plate a few quick swipes— more out of tradition than necessity. As bits of dust swirled off the hard rubber surface, he seemed satisfied with its newfound glimmer and returned the broom to its rightful place at his hefty side. He then rose and walked to his familiar position behind Mets catcher Clarence "Choo-Choo" Coleman, who, like the big umpire, was enjoying his third season of major-league baseball. With Paciorek looking on near the on-deck circle, Pryor shouted, "Play ball!"

With one out it was his turn. Paciorek, who had every reason to be nervous in his debut at-bat, crossed the white chalk line that marked out the right-hand side of the batter's box and dug in. Looking out toward Bearnarth, Pryor went into his umpire stance, one foot ahead of the other, front knee bent, rear leg mostly straight. Leaning forward as he was, with one leg a giant step in front of the other, it was easy to imagine a saber in Pryor's upraised hand as he charged out to do battle. This was no battle, however. This was the cellar-dwelling, tenth-place New York Mets versus the ninth-place Houston Colt .45s, a team that many years later Rusty Staub would describe on the home page of his Rusty Staub Foundation website as "terrible." If the ballpark was terrible, though, Paciorek, the man who would occupy right field on the final day of the 1963 season, was anything but.

"You can never understand how good an athlete he was," Staub said many years later. "He had it all, everything."[19]

For Paciorek, that wasn't enough. "I wanted to be the best there ever was," he said.

That season, neither the Colts nor the Mets were the best. Both teams were finishing their second seasons as expansion clubs, and both clearly needed expansion in the player personnel and run production departments if anything was to improve the following season. They would get little audible encouragement from the meager crowd of Texas partisans that day.

Not that crowd encouragement is necessary to inspire big-league ballplayers to great performances. Just nineteen months earlier, on March 2, 1962, seven-foot center Wilt Chamberlain had set a one-game National Basketball Association scoring mark that still stands. With only 4,124 people watching at the Hershey Sports Arena in Pennsylvania, Chamberlain poured in one hundred points. As Chamberlain sank point after point in a 169–147 win over the New York Knicks, you could practically hear a pin drop. Paciorek, playing before an even smaller crowd, was hearing the same kind of scattered applause that Chamberlain probably did.

As the home plate umpire, one of a crew of four officials who were calling the game that afternoon, Pryor served as the umpire in chief for the quartet. As such, he was not the crew chief, an honor that belonged to the most experienced of the four umpires—Frank Secory, a former outfielder who played six seasons with the Detroit Tigers, Cincinnati Reds, and Chicago Cubs before switching allegiances to umpire in the major leagues beginning in 1952. Ken Burkhart, number two in seniority that day, had begun his umpiring career five years after Secory and would handle third base; Frank Walsh, at second base, and Pryor, who both began umpiring at the professional level in 1961, were still cutting their teeth in the major leagues. On that afternoon Secory (at second base), Burkhart, and Walsh would work the base paths while Pryor as "quarterback" called balls and strikes.

Despite his inexperience, Pryor had solid tools, both umpiring and otherwise. At the ripe old age of thirty-six, the Rhode Island native had been a minor-league pitcher for three seasons in the 1940s after graduating from High Point College, a private liberal arts school in North Carolina. After coaching football and baseball in Wisconsin and North Carolina for several years he decided to try his hand at umpiring, working in the Georgia State League, Tri-State League, Carolina League, Sally League, and American Association before earning a coveted promotion to the major leagues. Twenty years later, in 1981, he would retire from umpiring with impressive credentials on his curriculum vitae: He had umpired in three World Series and four All-Star games.

Perhaps better known nowadays than Paul Pryor the umpire is Paul Pryor the businessman, founder of Paul Pryor Travel Bags, Inc. During an off season several years into his career Pryor designed a bag used to carry umpiring equipment, then joined forces with a small manufacturing company in Florida that would make the bags. From there he started his own company, expanding it to include bags for baseball and football equipment, a special line of women's carry-on bags, and finally athletic equipment and corporate travel bags. A line of sportswear was eventually added to the product roster of Paul Pryor Travel Bags, whose corny motto continues to reflect the company's baseball—and, specifically, umpiring—origin despite the addition of non-umpire-related products: *Remember—you're "safe" with a Paul Pryor bag.*

To Paciorek, a native of Detroit, it didn't matter who was calling balls and strikes that afternoon or who had designed what kind of umpiring luggage. He had business to attend to and his own concerns to assuage, chief among them proving himself capable during his first at-bat. Paciorek believed the odds were in his favor. After all, he had strength and he had ability. And he had confidence.

"I believed I was probably as good as anyone, and I wanted to go out and prove that," he said, adding, "I always had that confident belief that I was destined to play in the major leagues. I felt I belonged there, that life and major-league baseball were intertwined."

The youngest player on the field that day and perhaps the least experienced of anyone on either team, Paciorek's reviews were mixed, although he had put up impressive numbers in the slugging department for the Class A Modesto Colts of the California League. Although hitting just .219 in seventy-eight games he had sixty hits, nine home runs, and forty-nine RBI at the time he was summoned to join the big club. He also had struck out ninety-four times in 274 at-bats, more than one strikeout every three times he came to the plate. Still, he was satisfied.

"It seemed like I was really having a good year, although I was horrible for a long period of time before I finally told them I was hurt," Paciorek said. "I started off pretty well, I know I was hitting over .300 at the beginning of the season. I was hitting home runs pretty easily as well as extra-base hits. It seemed like I was always on second base. It was in the middle of the season that I [first] got hurt. After that I was going back and forth [between Houston and Modesto] to get my back looked at by doctors."

Only one other Modesto teammate joined Paciorek in the Colt .45s' starting lineup that day: the diminutive Morgan, a little-known twenty-year-old second baseman who was hitting .263 with five home runs at the time he was called to Houston just nine days before Paciorek. At five foot seven and 160 pounds, Morgan's future in the major leagues was anything but secure, although while playing for

Houston's AA San Antonio Bullets the following season he was elevated to the Colts for good. Morgan, who went hitless that final afternoon of 1963, eventually played twenty-two seasons in the major leagues, most notably as a member of Cincinnati's Big Red Machine. He was elected to the Hall of Fame in 1990, finishing his career with a respectable 268 home runs and 1,133 RBI.

In addition to Paciorek and Morgan the lineup card also listed six other rookies who would go on to enjoy successful big-league careers. The redheaded Staub, Paciorek's Arizona Instructional League roommate in 1963 and perhaps the most notable of all starters that day—he would hit more career home runs than both Wynn and Morgan—had made his major-league debut the previous season, in April 1962, and ended up hitting .224 with six home runs and forty-five RBI for the Colts. He eventually would play twenty-three seasons in the major leagues with six different teams, and when he retired in 1985 Staub and Ty Cobb were the only players in the history of baseball to have hit home runs before turning twenty and after turning forty.

As Paciorek's roommate, Staub had a front-row seat to Paciorek's dithyrambic workout schedule, which included counting, clapping, and other annoyances. Peace and calm, it must have seemed to Staub, were anathema to the energetic Paciorek. At times, Paciorek, whom his brother Tom described as a "free spirit" but who was nicknamed "the flake" by teammates because of the ankle weights and weighted vest he wore and for his other exercise eccentricities, made Staub and others bristle with his high-octane energy.

"I was always hustling," said Paciorek, who compared himself to Cincinnati's Pete Rose, nicknamed "Charlie Hustle," and Washington Nationals spark plug Bryce Harper. "I would sprint on and off the field. I would back up everybody. I played very much like Pete Rose even before Rose became known for it. I didn't do it for show—I always wanted to be the best I could be."[20]

One day Staub had suffered enough from Paciorek's loud counting and clapping during early-morning calisthenics. Picking up a bat, he decided to take matters into his own hands:

> He was impossible as a young lad—he got up early in the morning, did exercises, and made noise. He was rooming with a veteran minor leaguer, Mike White, and they brought me in and asked if I would change roommates and take this young rookie. We got along awfully well once we had established rules: He could no longer count when he did his morning calisthenics, and he could no longer clap his hands. The counting and clapping ended when I came home one evening at about ten o'clock and he was asleep on the bed. I took a bat and started swinging it just above his head. It woke him up and he said, "What, are you crazy?" I said, "No crazier than you in the morning. Stop making noise. You do whatever you're gonna do and I'll deal with it. But you're not counting and you're not clapping!" We established some rules early and got along the whole time.

Like Staub, left fielder Wynn also started alongside Paciorek. Called up in July, Wynn would finish his first major-league season hitting under .250 with just four home runs and twenty-seven RBI. Over the next fifteen years he, too, would play for six different teams, although most of his tenure—eleven seasons—was spent with the Houston organization. While with the Colts and later the Astros, Wynn would earn a reputation as a solid a home run hitter, belting thirty or more round-trippers three times and twice knocking in one hundred or more runs. When the Astros traded him after the 1973 season he promptly slugged thirty-two home runs and drove in 108 RBI for his new team, the Dodgers, where he would play for three more seasons before once again moving on. At the time of his retirement Wynn was a classic journeyman ballplayer who had successfully plied his trade for five different teams.

Other rookies in the starting lineup that day were Ivan Murrell, who had yet to bat for the Colts that season but who went on to play ten seasons in the majors; John Bateman, who had ten home runs and fifty-nine RBI in 1963 and also spent a decade in the big leagues; and the pitcher Zachary, who, like Paciorek, broke in as a teenager and was 2 and 2 in 1963. Zachary played nine seasons in the major leagues, winning ten games and losing twenty-nine—unimpressive numbers by any measure. Nineteen-year-old Glenn Vaughan from Compton, California, was the eighth rookie in the starting lineup.

Of the eight rookies who started, only Paciorek and Glenn Vaughan, sometimes a shortstop, sometimes a third baseman, would fall out of the public eye. Called up to the Colt .45s along with Morgan, Vaughan played regularly during the last ten days of the season, smacking five hits but hitting only .167—numbers that failed to convince management of his prowess. Like Musial, Hubbs, Umbricht, and Paciorek, Vaughan would never again wear a major-league uniform, although for a very different reason: He simply wasn't good enough.

The only non-rookie in the starting lineup was Aspromonte, who opened at third base and went 2 for 4 with one RBI and three runs scored. Aspromonte, who was twenty-five at the time, must have felt like a patriarch of sorts. Then in his fifth season, Aspromonte, whose brother Ken was finishing up his career with Hubbs and the Cubs, would hit only .214 that season. His low batting average aside, he was the team leader that afternoon by virtue of age and experience, with eight rookies—several of them still teenagers—under his tutelage. His veteran status counted for something—he would play eight more seasons despite the low average in 1963, finishing with a respectable lifetime batting average of .252 with sixty home runs and 457 RBI.

Paciorek's .219 batting average notwithstanding, he did have success driving in runs at Modesto (he had forty-nine), and someone— perhaps owner Roy Hofheinz, whom Paciorek met only once, or his subaltern, manager Craft—must have figured he deserved a closer look and given the nod for him to play against the Mets. Or perhaps the credit goes to general manager Richards, whose tall, slender frame and slicked-back grayish-black hair reminded Paciorek of a Spanish don—"and everyone treated him like one, too," he said. Some have speculated that the innovative Richards, who genuinely liked Paciorek, may have influenced both Hofheinz and Craft in an effort to bolster his youth movement, although Paciorek believes it ultimately may have been Pat Gillick, who was new to the front office in 1963, or pitching coach Ellis "Cot" Deal who carried out instructions to offer him a chance at playing—he doesn't recall who the messenger was. Whatever the reason, and whoever was involved, a look was what Paciorek got, albeit a short one. A glance. A wink. A big-league blip.

"There had to be some kind of relationship [involved in calling him up]," Aspromonte speculated. "If you bring somebody up you bring him up September 1. Someone did a favor, but at the same time [Paciorek] really produced for that favor."

Whatever got him there, whatever paved the way for him to make the big club with less than a season of Class A ball under his belt, whatever convinced the powers that be that the eighteen-year-old wouldn't embarrass himself or the organization with this giant leap forward, Paciorek, the youngest player on the Modesto Colts, was determined to make a success of his big-league debut. Standing in his way was a big bear, a man who wanted nothing less than to spoil the kid's big day: pitcher Bearnarth, a six-foot-two, 203-pound right-hander and himself a promising rookie. In the biggest of all pools, where a big, square-jawed, good-looking pitcher like Bearnarth who looked intimidating and could serve the ball with authority had a distinct advantage over a fresh-faced rookie just called up from the low minor leagues, Paciorek was poised to raise eyebrows as the lead curiosity in newspapers across the country the next morning. While the day would belong to retiring legend Musial, one of the greatest players ever to swing a bat, Stan the Man would have to share the spotlight with a relative unknown who on that day would establish a mark that promised to amaze the baseball world for months to come—until opening day the following season, when Paciorek would be noticeably absent from the starting lineup.

4

Batter Up

You only have to bat 1.000 in two things: flying and heart transplants. Everything else, you can go 4 for 5.
—*Carroll Hoff "Beano" Cook, historian*

Lindsey Nelson: Two men out and a runner at first and John Paciorek is coming up for his first time in the major leagues. Paciorek is eighteen years of age, six foot two, a two-hundred-pounder from Detroit, Michigan. He hit .219 in seventy-eight games at Modesto this season with nine homers and forty-nine runs batted in. Swings and sends a foul ball high into the air to the right side, into the stands and out of play.

With his first swing at a pitch from Bearnarth, in the second inning, shortly after 4 p.m. Central Time, on September 29, 1963, at Colt Stadium, John Paciorek shed a sigh of relief. He would not suffer the perceived indignity, which it really wouldn't have been, of a called strike on the first pitch of his big-league career. There would be no swinging strike, either, no chasing after a bad pitch in the dirt, or one that sailed high and in above the letters, or one that missed the corner as it swooshed down and away off the outer edge of home plate. His youthful zeal would not shortchange Paciorek as his new teammates looked on with mild interest at his fast ascent. He did not want to fail himself, and he did not want to fail the home fans, either, most of whom had never heard his name before. Sure, Paciorek didn't greet Bearnarth by lashing his first pitch for a single up the middle between second baseman Ron Hunt and shortstop Al Moran, or by dropping a base hit down the third base line and over the head of Jim Hickman, or by driving a double deep into the gap between center fielder Duke Carmel and left fielder Hicks. However, he did get a piece of the ball—enough to send it drifting into the stands along the first base side and giving someone an early souvenir, one that today might bring a modest yield on the auction block.

"I know what I *would* have been thinking: I'm just ready to hit at anything," Paciorek said of that first pitch. "If I fouled it off it's because I was looking for a strike. I wasn't thinking too technically at that particular time—I wanted to get in there, look for the ball and hit it. Later, I may have been trying to find the slot where [Bearnarth] was releasing the ball, but I really wasn't thinking of that then. I wanted to hit anything that was close."

Paciorek got just enough of the ball to give himself some needed confidence as he strove to find his footing with a new team, in a new league and at a level he wasn't accustomed to. *I can hit this guy,* he thought to himself. Why wouldn't he think that?

"I knew [that] was the only place for me," he said, describing what it felt like to play in a major-league game for the first time. "I had dreamed of it all my life."[21]

Later on, in the fourth, fifth, and eighth innings, he would prove to the few fans in attendance at the rickety, single-level stadium, which was situated on a slice of prairie near downtown Houston, that indeed it was the only place for him, that he could play baseball in the major leagues—and that he could play it better than anyone else on either team that particular day.

Nelson: Here's a pitch inside for a ball.

As he waited patiently for a pitch he could hit, Paciorek showed a quality that would serve him well that day: patience. He was focused on hitting the baseball and was willing to wait for a pitch in the right spot. He would swing at any ball that was close to the strike zone as long as it was hittable, and for most of the day he took advantage of the good pitches that came his way while laying off the bad ones. Paciorek wanted a base hit, and he wasn't about to swing at sucker pitches, which could send him back to the dugout with his confidence shaken and Craft mumbling epithets sotto voce. If he were to strike out it would be harder to hit the next time up, especially if he swung at a bad pitch or two to help Bearnarth pick up the "K." Like center fielder Murrell, the previous batter. In his first major-league at-bat, with one out and Aspromonte on first base following a walk, Murrell, who was twenty, struck out on three straight pitches, two of them called strikes. Perhaps Paciorek learned something by observing the lanky Murrell. In sharp contrast, he would wait on thirteen balls that afternoon, receiving two walks. But as playground players have said almost since the days of Abner Doubleday, and as Paciorek and his friends probably chanted in the heat of battle many times on the school yard or open fields where pieces of plywood or sections of newspaper served as bases, a walk is as good as a hit. If that was true then Paciorek would go 5 for 5—not 3 for 3—on that sultry autumn afternoon.

Nelson: That pitch is outside for a ball, it's 2 and 1.

Ahead on the count, Paciorek sensed he was inching toward another milestone: his first time on base. Were that to occur a number of possibilities would arise, including a chance for the fleet-footed rookie to steal a base and eventually score a run. There would be several opportunities for Paciorek to run the bases that day, and many chances to drive in his teammates.

"Nobody was stronger than he was, and no one could hit a ball harder or farther than he could," Tom Paciorek said. "John was an amazing athlete."

Tom added, laughing, "He was a better athlete—I was a better player. John could've and should've been much better. He had the capability of being a star on a team, even on a major-league team. If you talk with Joe Morgan and Jim Wynn, they'll tell you that, too. John had the capability of being the number three or number four hitter on a good major-league team."

His physical attributes notwithstanding, at that moment first base, ninety feet from where he stood with catcher Coleman and umpire Pryor crouched close behind him, might as well have been miles away, and it probably looked as distant to him as San Jacinto Monument or the Alamo. For John Paciorek, a base hit in his first major-league at-bat was still the objective, not a base on balls. Considering the rookie's lack of playing experience, a hit was a long shot.

Nelson: Now the 2-and-1 pitch is outside for a ball.

With the count in his favor Paciorek was sizing up Bearnarth pitch by pitch. He wanted to help construct a rally, but he wasn't about to squander a possible walk by trying too hard. He was one pitch away from his first chance to run the bases and move Aspromonte into scoring position. If he failed to get a hit, if he found himself on base with a walk, perhaps he would get his first hit the next time around, in the fourth or fifth inning. For every player, a chance to improve on the previous at-bat is always only an inning or two away.

Nelson: Here's a swing and a ground ball foul.

With the count full Paciorek's stomach was churning with anticipation. His first at-bat was grinding on, almost in slow motion— five pitches so far—and he had taken the pitcher all the way. He had fouled off two pitches, showing Bearnarth he was capable of getting wood on the ball—or at least slivers. He had also watched three bad ones go by for balls, showing a keen eye for the strike zone. The next pitch would likely put him on first with a feeling of exhilaration or send him back to the bench, disappointed or disillusioned. Either way, he was getting a whiff of the highs and lows of playing in the major leagues. With their own careers winding to a close, Musial and Hubbs, who by then were also playing in their final games as big leaguers, had both become accustomed to the ups and downs of big-league baseball, as had Jim Umbricht, who would pitch his final fraction of an inning later on in the game.

Nelson: Here's a pitch high, and going on down to first is Paciorek with a base on balls. So he has walked his first time up in the major leagues.

As he flung aside his bat, Paciorek sped down the first base line like a man on fire. He later wrote why he didn't believe in slow-trotting down the line like many other ballplayers did.

"When the superb base runner receives a base-on-balls he sprints to first base for the purpose of . . . warming and readying his body for the new prospective confrontations—especially if he is a base stealing threat," he explained in his book.[22]

As he touched the puffy, scuffed bag for the first time in his career Paciorek barely had time to think ahead to the next batter, or the next potential game situation. Three pitches later catcher Bateman would blast a triple over right fielder Kranepool's head, the ball one-hopping the wall and sending the National League's newest rookie sprinting on the heels of Aspromonte and all the way around from first to score his first major-league run. It is not surprising that he ran well and enjoyed running the bases.

"Running the bases is one of the most fun and exciting parts of the game," Paciorek wrote in his book. "The good or great base runner is . . . determined to make something positive happen when he makes ball contact at the plate or is already on base. His is a totally greedy attitude from which resonates the obvious message that to him belongs sole possession of each and every base he makes the effort to encounter."[23]

Less than two innings into his debut game Paciorek had proven himself a worthy rookie, nailing down his first pair of putouts, getting on base for the first time, and scoring his first big-league run.

As he caught his breath and danced down into the dugout Paciorek was pleased. His uniform, bearing the number 22, was now wrinkled, perspiration was building, his legs were warm from running the bases, and he was getting his feet wet as a member of the Colt .45s in a big way. Henry Workman, whose major-league career lasted just two games with the 1950 New York Yankees, knows how Paciorek felt at having made it to the major leagues, if only for a nano-season. "It means a lot," said the former pinch hitter/first baseman, who went 1 for 5 in his brief "career" to finish with a "lifetime" batting average of .200. "You don't think you're going up for [just] a brief period."

As Paciorek took his place on the Colt bench, his first plate appearance safely in the books, the right-hander Zachary stepped to the plate for his first at-bat of the ball game. There was much more baseball to play, and Paciorek was itching to bring it on.

5

Yo-Yo

*I never want to quit playing ball. They'll have to cut
this uniform off of me to get me out of it.*
—Roy Campanella, catcher

Unlike Brooklyn Dodgers catcher Roy Campanella, whose career
ended when an automobile accident left him paralyzed from his
muscular, home-run-hitting shoulders on down, catcher Aubrey
Epps went into retirement from major-league baseball without even
knowing he was through—after just one game. Next to Paciorek,
the slender backstop with the thick southern drawl has the honor
of owning the second best single-game career in baseball history.
Still, Epps, who accomplished the feat as a member of the Depression-era Pittsburgh Pirates, is a mystery man. For more than a generation, from September 29, 1935, until Paciorek eclipsed his
standing atop the pack in 1963, Epps arguably remained head and
shoulders above everyone else who had the distinction of playing in
only one major-league game, posting a .750 batting average and becoming the first one-game wonder to record three base hits; with
Paciorek in the club there now are two players with three hits in

their only major-league game. Epps attained the number one position by going 3 for 4 in the second game of a doubleheader against the Cincinnati Reds on the final day of the 1935 season, although despite his offensive productivity the Pirates lost the nightcap, 9–6. Then he, like Paciorek nearly three decades after him, disappeared from the big-league baseball radar screen—until now.

Epps was quickly forgotten after his one game in the spotlight, suffering a fate slightly worse than Paciorek, whose accomplishment also was hidden for many years but is now becoming known across the baseball landscape—thanks in large part to the Internet and its ability to spread fame and notoriety and the growing legion of writers who have chronicled his achievement. That Epps's name doesn't roll off the tongue as easily as Paciorek's is probably because in 1935 there were few readily available compendia of statistical information that baseball junkies could pore through to find such obscure results. *The Baseball Encyclopedia*, which beginning in 1969 was the undisputed Bible for baseball statisticians, was not even a dream when Epps played ball. Its eventual publication was largely due to the efforts of Lee Allen, former historian for the Baseball Hall of Fame in Cooperstown, New York, and John Tattersall, an executive with a Philadelphia steamship company who himself was a historian who cherished the possibility of developing a thorough baseball reference and, along with Allen, made it happen.[24] By the time *The Baseball Encyclopedia* was first cranked into print, Epps's accomplishment was a footnote hidden in the tiniest of type. Buried snugly within the book's nearly three thousand pages, Epps never would become a baseball trivia question until someone was willing to spend the time and eyestrain to navigate that massive volume of diminutively posted statistics, standings, and other data, a prodigious feat.

Not even Richard Tellis, who years after the first article on Paciorek appeared in the *Los Angeles Times* completed the quirky *Once Around the Bases*, a nifty book that chronicles the one-game careers of forty players whose tenures in baseball were gnat-like in scope, included a chapter on the now-venerable Epps, nicknamed Yo-Yo due to his skill with the then-popular toy. He does, however, include mini biographies on Paciorek as well as Merritt Lovett, Manuel Onis, Harry Chozen, Pinson McCullough, LeRoy Talcott Jr., Otis Davis, and Laverne Holtgrave—hardly household names.

Born March 3, 1912 in Memphis, Tennessee, Epps graduated from long-defunct Memphis Tech High School, whose roster of famous alumni includes singer Kay Starr ("Wheel of Fortune," "Rock and Roll Waltz") and former Brooklyn Dodger and Philadelphia Phillie Bobby Bragan, before signing with the Class A Birmingham Barons of the Southern Association and thus entering the hardscrabble world of Depression-era minor-league baseball. At age twenty-one in 1933 he batted .225 for the Barons and was sent down to the Class C Longview Cannibals of the Dixie League, where in six games he hit .318. The following season he returned to Birmingham, where Barons manager Clyde Milan moved him to center field, probably with the expectation of getting more power out of his young prospect. Epps responded favorably by hitting .301 with 170 hits, including 24 doubles and 11 triples—his propensity to hit triples was unusual for a born-and-bred catcher, and his one game in the major leagues would include a triple as well as two singles.

On September 1, toward the end of the 1934 season, the Pittsburgh Pirates acquired the catcher-turned-center-fielder for an undisclosed amount of money. His arrival was highly anticipated according to one newspaper, which ran a banner headline in its sports section: "Pirates Pay Cash for Birmingham Catcher." The subhead read, "Youngster Is Great Prospect in Only Third Year of Baseball":

The Pirates reached into the Southern Association yesterday to pluck a promising young catcher for trial next spring. Upon the unqualified recommendation of Carleton Molesworth, veteran Southern ivory comber, the Pittsburgh club purchased Aubrey Epps from Birmingham. He will remain with the Barons for the remainder of the season and don Pirate spangles for the first time in training camp at San Bernardino, Cal., next March.

Epps, who is only 21 years old, is playing his third season in professional baseball and is regarded as one of the best young prospects in his league. There was a wild scramble to purchase his contract, the Pirates outbidding the Cleveland Indians to land him. President Bill Benswanger announced the deal as a straight cash transaction and the Pirates will not have to send any players to Birmingham. Epps' price tag was not announced.

The new Pirate is a combination outfielder-catcher. Pressed for gardeners this spring, Birmingham used Epps in the outfield, but he has been behind the plate in about 50 games. Upon his purchase by the Pirates, the Birmingham club was notified that the youngster must be used solely as a catcher for the remainder of the season. In other words, the Pirates, in rebuilding for 1935, are not so much worried about outfield talent as they are catchers.

Epps at present owns a batting average of .307.[25]

Despite hitting over .300 as an outfielder and demonstrating that by casting aside the wear and tear caused by crouching for nine innings he could actually swing a bat for extra bases, Epps, as promised, was used exclusively as a catcher for the rest of the season.

Expectations were again high the following year and it was believed that Epps might start the 1935 season on the Pittsburgh roster, but it was not to be. He was returned to Birmingham, one of the oldest minor-league franchises in baseball.

Established in 1885 as the Birmingham Coal Barons, the team originally played at a site indecorously called Slag Pile, near the Alabama Great Southern Railroad tracks. However, as the team became established, plans were developed in 1901 to build the first steel-and-concrete ballpark in the short history of minor-league baseball: Richwood Field. A consultant on the project was none other than Connie Mack, famed manager of the Philadelphia Athletics from 1901 through his retirement in 1950.

The Barons set several attendance records during the 1920s and continued strong as they entered the Depression, winning the Southern Association pennant in 1931. Unfortunately, that was the team's high-water mark for the remainder of the decade, which included Epps's several stints with the Barons in the mid-1930s. His best average was .324, which he recorded in 1935 before joining the Fort Worth Cats of the Texas League, where his average slumped to .203. Epps's overall history of up-and-down offensive play apparently failed to discourage management: He was elevated to the Pirates, the fourth team he would play for that year, for the final game of the 1935 season, where he made baseball history in the unlikeliest fashion.

Up until that point Epps's minor-league numbers, although unpredictable, had been credible: In three seasons he had hit .287 with 364 hits, fifty doubles, and an incredible twenty-nine triples. It may have been the extra-base hits, especially the three-baggers, that caught the attention of Pittsburgh management and convinced them to give the speedy catcher a shot with the Pirates—he had averaged nearly seventeen doubles and ten triples per season before making his way to the big club at the end of the 1935 campaign. Whatever the reason, Epps was behind the plate for Game 2 of the September 29, 1935, doubleheader against Cincinnati, replacing error-prone Tom Padden following his solid 3-for-4 performance in the first game, which the Pirates won, 5–1.

During that game, Epps, hitting eighth in the batting order, came to bat four times, slugged a triple and two singles (matching Paciorek's three hits), drove in three runs (also matching Paciorek), and scored a run (three fewer than Paciorek). His two errors behind the plate were two more than Paciorek, who was perfect in the outfield, would make. Epps also recorded six putouts, all resulting from rookie starting pitcher Claude Passeau's one strikeout in three innings worked (Passeau, a look-alike for actor Gregory Peck, was also making his major-league debut that day) and relief pitcher Ralph Birkofer's five strikeouts.

After the game Epps likely received considerable media attention, much as Paciorek did in 1963, but he wasn't able to bask in the accolades for long. An October 31, 1935, Associated Press article tells the story of what happened to Epps beginning three weeks after the completion of the Pirates 1935 season, probably around October 21:

(AP)—Aubrey Epps, 21-year-old catcher of the Pittsburgh Pirates, battled for his life in a hospital (in Memphis) tonight, weak from the ravages of pneumonia.

His illness developed from a cold following a tonsillectomy nine days ago.

Epps began his baseball career with Birmingham of the Southern Association and was purchased by Pittsburgh at the end of his first season. He was sent back to Birmingham last year for further seasoning and later was transferred to Fort Worth of the Texas League. He was recalled by the Pirates late in the summer.

Hopeful of landing a first-string catching berth with Pittsburgh next season, Epps decided to start getting in condition early by having his tonsils removed about nine days ago.

Hemorrhages caused him to return to the hospital two days later. A severe cold, which impaired his breathing, developed into pneumonia.[26]

Epps's story, which he related to this writer shortly before succumbing, concurred with that account. "I came down with pneumonia after the game and got pretty sick," he said in our 1982 interview. "I never got back to where I was physically at the end of that season. I never got back to the major leagues again."

At one point during his "recovery" it was doubtful whether Epps would survive. However, survive he did, recovering in time to compete for a spot on the Pirates' 1936 opening-day roster. Epps did not make the team and spent the season with the Class A Scranton

Miners of the New York–Pennsylvania League, where he hit a career high .332 and showed management he was still a force to be reckoned with. Down, at least for the 1936 campaign as far as the Pittsburgh Pirates were concerned, Epps was far from out, as the Associated Press pointed out in a footnote to the 1935 season:

> (AP)—The Pirates' hospital list is being rubbed out and [manager] Pie Traynor is glad. Hal Finney, out for a year with bad eyes, is on the way for a comeback as catcher, while Aubrey Epps, also a catcher, seems to have recovered fully from a siege of pneumonia.

The article followed a similar piece in the *Pittsburgh Post-Gazette*, dated December 31, 1935. *The Post-Gazette* brief must have given fans a dose of hope:

> Catcher Aubrey Epps, who was stricken with pneumonia and subsequently suffered a relapse, has just written to President Bill Benswanger stating that he was dismissed from the hospital after nine days of treatment on his second visit to the institution and now is improving steadily at his home in Memphis. His physician advises him to take matters slowly and not venture out of the house until the weather moderates. He expects to be able to report at training time.[27]

That was the peak for Epps, who had high hopes for making the team. He did not. Instead, he spent the 1936 season with his old club, the Scranton Miners, the 1937 season with the Memphis Chickasaws of the Southern Association, 1938 with the Jackson Senators of the Southeastern League, 1939 with Memphis again, 1940 with the Jersey City Giants of the International League, and 1941 with the Milwaukee Brewers of the American Association and the Knoxville Smokies of the Southern Association. His best season was 1936 when he hit .332 with twenty-two doubles and eight triples, although he did hit .305 for Knoxville in 1941, slugging fourteen home runs. Epps retired in 1941 with a whopping fifty-one triples to his credit in nine minor-league seasons, an unheard-of number for a catcher and even for much swifter players by today's standards. Now resting in relative obscurity, Epps remains a footnote to Paciorek's historic legacy.

Aubrey Epps. (Jim Rowe baseball card)

6

One for One

I would have been batting 1.000, except for the strikeouts—
if there were no fielders out there.
—*Delmon Young, outfielder*

Ralph Kiner: The bases [are] loaded, no one out, the batter is John Paciorek. John Paciorek walked his first time up, he takes outside—ball one. He's a right-hand batter. He, too, looking for his first major-league hit. Officially, he has not been at bat, although he has walked one time.

Watching from the broadcast booth as Paciorek stepped to the plate for his second at-bat, Ralph McPherran Kiner may have visualized himself seventeen seasons earlier when he made his own major-league debut on April 16, 1946. Both men stood six foot two and weighed a formidable two hundred pounds, both batted and threw right-handed, and both played right field, although Kiner also spent time in left field and at first base. Within minutes Kiner would watch as Paciorek, buoyed by an unusual level of confidence for such a young man, smacked his first base hit—a Texas Leaguer—much as he, Kiner, had done many times during his breakout rookie season. Both men would ultimately retire from the game they loved because of back injuries.

Playing for the Pittsburgh Pirates as a twenty-three-year-old sensation out of Alhambra High School, which is situated less than five miles from where Paciorek lives today, Kiner collected 124 hits as a first-year player, 23 of them home runs, and drove in eighty-one runs. His batting average was only .247, and he did strike out 109 times (more than once every five at bats), but his numbers were good enough to earn him a few nods in the National League Most Valuable Player balloting.

The following season Kiner corrected his rookie shortcomings, including a propensity to strike out and his low batting average. He hit .313 in 1947, the highest batting average he would ever record, while blasting fifty-one home runs and driving in 127 runners. Perhaps most notable, in nearly a hundred additional at-bats he struck out twenty-eight fewer times. Despite leading the league in home runs Kiner placed only sixth in the National League MVP voting, which was won by long-forgotten Bob Elliott of the Boston Braves, a teammate of Kiner during the 1946 season. In winning the MVP award Elliott's numbers paled in comparison with Kiner's, as he hit only twenty-two home runs, drove in 113 runners, and batted just four points higher at .317.

Although Kiner's career was shortened by injury—he was forced to retire after ten seasons—his offensive statistics were still exceptional. The six-time All-Star, who played three seasons with the Chicago Cubs at the end of his career, slugged 369 home runs, drove in 1,015 RBI, and compiled a .279 lifetime batting average. He was elected to the baseball Hall of Fame in 1975—twenty years after he left the game.

Unlike many players, Kiner's retirement in 1955 did not mark the end of his baseball career. In 1961 he was hired by the Chicago White Sox to join its broadcast team, and a year later, while Paciorek was wrapping up his junior year in high school and perhaps planning for the upcoming prom, he moved over to the Mets as a broadcaster. During the decades after he began calling Mets games alongside veteran announcer Nelson, Kiner methodically rose to achieve legend status, due as much to his longevity as to his ability to announce baseball games. His fifty-two consecutive seasons calling games for the same team ranked him third among active broadcasters at the time of his death, behind only Vin Scully of the Dodgers, who had completed sixty-three seasons, and the team's Spanish-language announcer, Jaime Jarrin, who entered the club's broadcast booth in 1958—the team's first year in Los Angeles. When he died in 2014, Kiner was the oldest active broadcaster in baseball and a true legend.

As he helped Nelson call the action that fall afternoon Kiner was nearly as inexperienced as the rookie Paciorek. In just his third season he was splitting time behind the mic with Nelson, who had broken into broadcasting fifteen years earlier, and was calling the action every third inning; he holds the distinction of having announced Paciorek's first major-league hit—something he did not recall: "I don't know anything about him," he said.

Nelson, who also broke in with the Mets in 1962, spent seventeen seasons with the team—one-third the number of years that Kiner was with the club. At his induction into the broadcasters' wing of the Baseball Hall of Fame in 1988, Nelson paid Kiner and the third member of the broadcast team, Bob Murphy, who passed away

Appearing dapper at the St. Ladislaus High School senior prom, 1962

in 2004, the ultimate tribute: "Sometimes, when I'm in bed, I hear a voice that says, 'Hello everybody, this is Lindsey Nelson along with Bob Murphy and Ralph Kiner from Shea Stadium in New York.'"[28]

Throughout the history of major-league baseball dozens of players have left the game with a batting average of 1.000. Most went 1 for 1 in a single game, then drifted into anonymity. A handful ended their careers with two hits in two at-bats, gaining slightly more ex-posure.[29] As September 29, 1963 unfolded, none had batted 1.000 with three base hits, something that would soon change.

Certainly, Paciorek had no intention of becoming a one-game wonder, then swiftly falling out of the public eye as many of his baseball forebears, including Epps, had done. He was at Colt Sta-dium to begin a long and productive career, and nothing would keep him from achieving that goal—not hard-throwing right-handers like Bearnarth nor his own dearth of experience nor the back injury that continued to plague him, although on that day he managed to dis-miss the pain from his parietal lobe. The base hits would come in time, the health-conscious-yet-hard-hitting Paciorek reassured him-self. Sharing that assessment was Paul Runge, a Modesto teammate.

"He was a big-time athlete, in very good shape—he looked like a million bucks to me," said Runge, who failed to make the big leagues as a player but later spent twenty-four seasons as a National League umpire. "He ate the right foods, and at that age not too many of us did that.

"We used to eat at those all-you-can-eat restaurants and they'd serve prime rib. I can remember him cutting off little, thin pieces of fat—he wouldn't eat any fat." Runge described Paciorek as "a real nice guy, very athletic, very straight, good looking."

Raymond Ferrand, who played alongside Paciorek at Modesto and Durham and in spring training prior to the 1964 season, had similar recollections.

"He was a nice guy, real quiet, and he always talked about how good his brother [Tom] was," he said. "He didn't particularly care for the food they served in spring training, so he had his food catered in. He had signed for a pretty good bonus, I think, and I guess he had the money to do what he wanted to do."

According to onetime roommate Rusty Staub, Paciorek's eating habits eventually got him into trouble with the Miners Shack restaurant in Apache Junction, Arizona, where Arizona Instructional League players regularly ate. "He was the most voracious eater I have ever seen in my entire life," Staub said. "[The Miners Shack] served all you could eat for six or seven bucks, and they literally banned him from the restaurant—they would not let him come in. I've never seen anyone in such great shape eat so much food." Although his brother Tom corroborated Staub's story, Paciorek said his reputation as a Miners Shack expellee was exaggerated—"I didn't get banned . . . nobody could've eaten that much," he said—although he did acknowledge eating huge meals as both a prep ballplayer and a professional, up to five sandwiches at a sitting. "Maybe eating so much and the added weight of the food put undue pressure someplace else in my body and had something to do with my back problems," he speculated.

Trailing 4–2 in the bottom half of the fourth inning, Houston threatened to tie the game and go ahead when the first three batters, Staub, Aspromonte, and Murrell, reached base with singles. Most noteworthy of the three was Murrell's poke, a bunt to third that marked his first major-league hit. With the bases loaded, would Paciorek, who in the Mets half of the fourth inning warmed for this at-bat by cleanly fielding a line-drive single to right by first baseman Tim Harkness, take Murrell's lead and also record his first major-league hit, driving in one or two runs in the process? With a 1–0 count on him it wouldn't take long to find out.

Kiner: There's a little blooper into left field, a base hit. Coming in from third base is Rusty Staub. On second base is Bob Aspromonte, the throw is cut off and the Colt .45s have tied it up. John Paciorek getting his first major-league hit, which drove in two runs to tie the score at 4–4.

At the major-league level neither the velocity nor the trajectory of a hit is necessarily important, and a blooper over shortstop is as good as a single lined on a bounce to the left fielder. No matter what the angle of the baseball was, or how hard it was smacked, Paciorek would gladly have taken it, and he scurried down the first base line with a single in his pocket. The boy from Detroit via Hamtramck was now a major-league hitter in every sense of the word.

"I'd driven myself hard to reach that goal, devoting every ounce of my energy to get into the big leagues," he recalled.[30]

Paciorek felt spirited with his first major-league hit in the books, although Kiner said little about it as the ball dropped down and gently kissed the grass—only that the ball fell in untouched and that two runs scored as a result, tying the game at 4–4 and giving Paciorek a chance to run the bases again.

"Bases loaded, I was probably excited," Paciorek said. "I was probably thinking I wanted to hit the ball hard. That was fun."

Moments later, when Bearnarth gave up a hit to Bateman that scored Murrell and moved Paciorek over to second, Houston overtook the Mets to lead the game 5–4. Bauta was promptly summoned to replace Bearnarth, and he wasted little time giving up a bunt single to pinch hitter Al Spangler that sent Paciorek hustling over to third, loading the bases for the second time in the inning.

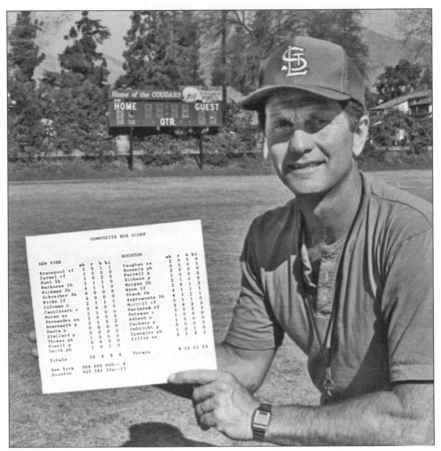

Posing with box score from his one and only major league game,
1991. (Photo by Steven K. Wagner)

"I knew [Paciorek] was in the same organization, I don't recall playing with him," said Spangler, who played for four major-league teams during a twelve-year career that ended in 1971. "I think he was tall and a right-handed hitter . . . I certainly remember the name." When told how well Paciorek played that day the gentlemanly Texan added, "I would say that's probably one of the best" single-game careers in history.

With Paciorek on third and veteran Pete Runnels coming up to pinch-hit for the short-timer Vaughan, Kiner continued calling the action from his perch off the playing field:

> **Kiner:** He hits the first pitch to deep right field, Eddie Kranepool waiting there with glasses down. Tags up, the runner at third base—he comes in to score after the catch, and moving over to third base is Johnny Bateman. Scoring from third base is John Paciorek.

As the game reached the midway point the sun was already becoming an obstacle in the outfield, and Kiner noted as much: Kranepool's glasses were already down as Runnels's fly ball headed toward him, and he was battling a glare that outfielders had come to expect in Houston. Kranepool's problem with the sun surprised no one, as Colt Stadium had a reputation for unbearable heat. During its brief existence the stadium was known as one of the hottest anywhere. Until evening, when the mosquitoes came out. "I don't care what ballpark they ever talk about as being the hottest place on the face of the earth, Colt Stadium was it," Staub once said.[31]

Paciorek felt the same way—about Colt Stadium *and* about Houston. "I would check my mail at the [Surrey House] motor hotel where the team stayed, and by the time I got back inside I'd have to change clothes. No matter what, it was humid."

Colt Stadium was barely a glimmer when Houston was awarded a National League franchise in 1960. Once that occurred, the team rushed to build a temporary stadium for use until construction of a permanent ballpark could be completed. Despite other monikers through the years, including the Reliant Astrodome, the ballpark would forever be known as, simply, the Astrodome, and it served as a template for other domed stadiums that would later be built to protect teams from the elements, mostly heat and rain, during a long baseball season that spanned parts of three seasons: spring, summer, and fall.

Built for a whopping $2 million, the Colts' first home was unusual in that it had just one tier of seats from foul pole to foul pole; there were no seats above the box level. Perhaps that explains the heat: Because there were no upper tiers to block the sun's rays and at least cool the lower-level seats, everyone and everything baked continuously until the sun went down—and the bugs came out. During the Colts' early years the heat at Colt Stadium became the stuff that legends are made of. Once, over the course of a Sunday doubleheader, more than one hundred people received treatment in the Colt Stadium first-aid facility, many, presumably, due to heat-related problems. "It wasn't *sort of* [hot], it was *very* hot," Spangler said of Colt Stadium, underscoring the ballpark's reputation as a sweat box.

The new ballpark contained thirty-three thousand seats, a scant number by the standards of today but probably considered sufficient for an expansion club that was not expected to win many games or sustain a large following of fans, at least in the early years. A single tier of colored seats stretched from the left field foul pole to home plate, swung around the backstop, then ran on out to the right field foul pole; seats also were available beyond the right field and left field fences, and a scoreboard was situated in dead center field. The field dimensions remained unchanged during the Colts' three seasons playing there: 400 feet to left field and right field and a ghastly 450 feet to dead center. While akin to a college or minor-league stadium in certain respects, Colt Stadium resembled the Polo Grounds, where the Mets would play until April 17, 1964, in one particular way: the vast distance to dead center field, which made home runs to that section of the ballpark a rarity. In comparison, center field at the Polo Grounds, a veritable no-man's-land, was 483 feet from home plate, space enough to accommodate Willie Mays as he burned into the minds of fans an image of himself making an over-the-head catch of a ball hit by Vic Wertz of the Baltimore Orioles in the 1954 World Series.

The first game played at Colt Stadium was on April 10, 1962, and with its many shortcomings the facility wasn't in use for very long. The final game was played on September 27, 1964, and by then Paciorek and his exploits were long forgotten. The stadium, too, would soon be forgotten, thanks in part to owner Hofheinz. Perhaps to hasten the stadium's disuse, Hofheinz had it painted gray to camouflage the ballpark in aerial photographs taken of the Astrodome, which could be seen beyond the first base grandstand at Colt Stadium. If he'd had a magic wand, Hofheinz probably would have made the ballpark disappear altogether.

A native Texan, Hofheinz was well known throughout the Lone Star State. He had served as a state representative when Bob Wills was establishing the Texas Playboys, from 1934 to 1936, and was a judge in Harris County for eight years after that, until 1944. He later served as the mayor of Houston from 1953 to 1955, where his reputation as a man capable of getting things done was solidified and where his support among the baseball populace continued to grow.

In 1960, "The Judge," as he was known, became a key figure in an effort to bring major-league baseball to Houston. While funding and organizational support had already been captured, a domed stadium was needed if Houston was to obtain one of two new franchises. With his broad background as a politician, judge, and businessman, Hofheinz was the man to get the job done.

With help from others, Hofheinz secured bond approval from Houston, where by then he was well known, to build what eventually would become the world-famous Astrodome. The price tag? More than $30 million. The franchise was awarded to Houston on October 17, 1960, and the Colt .45s were born eighteen months after that. Hofheinz wasted little time initiating construction of Colt Stadium adjacent to the Astrodome's eventual site for one very specific reason: He wanted fans to watch the ballpark rise. Along with that, he theorized, their enthusiasm for Houston baseball also would rise. The marketing ploy worked. Neither he nor the fans were disappointed as the Astrodome took shape behind Colt Stadium. You could almost hear the cranes swing into position as baseballs "popped" to the sound from nearby Colt Stadium.

Success came quickly for the Colts, although it was short-lived. In their debut game Houston beat the Cubs 11–2, with Aspromonte scoring the franchise's first run; the team would win only sixty-three more times in 1962. In its home debut Hubbs started at second base for the Cubs and went 0 for 4 during the game.

As owner of the Colts it was Hofheinz who eventually renamed the team the Astros, who gave the Astrodome its iconic name, and who was closely associated with the team during its first two years, which were largely marked by failure—the team won only sixty-six games in its second season. However, the larger picture stands as his hallmark, and on November 10, 2006, Hofheinz was inducted into the Texas Baseball Hall of Fame, where his formidable administrative heritage rests alongside baseball greats such as George "Sparky" Anderson, Hank Greenberg, Rogers Hornsby, Tris

Speaker, and Carl Hubbell.

As play moved to the Astrodome beginning in 1965, Colt Stadium remained a white elephant for five more seasons. After the Astrodome opened to great fanfare Colt Stadium was used primarily for storage, then was disassembled and sold to a minor-league baseball team in Mexico for the paltry sum of $100,000—just 5 percent of what it cost to build the stadium in 1961. Today, Colt Stadium is part of a public playground in Tampico, Mexico, where few people are probably aware of its brief, but significant, history as a major-league ballpark and precursor to the great Houston Astrodome.[32]

In baseball, as in other sports, sound fundamentals are critical to long-term success—ask any manager or veteran player, whose fortunes (salary and otherwise) rise and fall with good or bad rudimentary play. That's one area where rookies often fall short: They pay close attention to the big things, like hitting home runs and making marquee catches, in an effort to make a fast impression, while overlooking the little things. Often the most nuanced plays win ball games, especially close ones. One of the key rudiments in baseball is a player's ability to push a run across on an out, a passed ball, or even a strikeout. As Runnels went deep to right, Paciorek was focused, not musing about his first hit or basking in the glow of his budding success as a major-league ballplayer. He alertly tagged up at third as Kranepool made the easy catch looking into the sun. As the ball landed in the big right fielder's glove with a smack, Runnels rounded first, then headed back to the dugout. As Paciorek touched home plate, then returned to his spot on the bench, he was batting 1.000. He had earned his first major-league hit, had scored his first run, and the pieces were falling into place with what appeared to be relative ease. *This is fun*, he must have thought. On that day, up until that point in what was still a tight ballgame, it *had to have* been fun. With little preparation for what he was experiencing, and with minimal advance notice from the front office, Paciorek had stepped in with grace and found major-league baseball an easy transition— so far. As he watched his teammates bat around in the inning, with the runs piling up, Paciorek knew there would be more chances for him to secure his standing on the club before his first game was completed. That would prove to be an understatement.

7

The Man

How good was Stan Musial? He was good enough to
take your breath away.
—Vin Scully, broadcaster

St. Louis Cardinals announcer Harry Caray: Here's Musial, listen to the crowd again. A base hit would give the Cardinals the lead. First pitch—oh, what a cut he had and he fouled it back. Hey, he really had a swing at that one. Musial now at bat: 3,629 hits during his fabulous career. The stretch by [Jim] Maloney, slow curve [for a ball]. Take a good look, fans, take a good look. This might be the last time at bat in the major leagues. Remember the stance. And the swing. You're not likely to see his likes again. Fastball low and away, two balls and a strike. Stan got the first hit off Maloney, a single to center. The only other hit was a leadoff double by [Curt] Flood in the third. Two balls and a strike. The pitch to Musial: a hot shot on the ground into right field, a base hit. Here's Flood around third—no throw, the Cardinals lead 1–0. Listen to the crowd, listen to the crowd. Let's see now—manager Johnny Keene is talking to Gary Kolb, Stan is at first base, they might be waiting for the applause on the hit to die down. They'll tear the joint apart when he trots off the field. He would have gone out the way he came in, with a base hit. His first [career] base hit gave the Cardinals a 3–2 victory. Now listen, Gary Kolb is going to replace Musial. There he goes, the end of a great career.

With rookie-like exuberance and a bounce in his step, Stanislaus Frank Musial approached the batter's box at Busch Memorial Stadium from the left side and strode with deliberation into the narrow chalk rectangle that reached out toward the pitching mound. He leaned into a crouch, right knee tilted slightly inward, just as he'd done during each of more than 12,500 official and unofficial at-bats over twenty-one seasons with the St. Louis Cardinals. At about the same time, some eight hundred miles to the south, in a city—Houston—that in 1963 was relatively new to major-league baseball, Paciorek was doing the same thing: coming to bat in the sixth inning. There was great disparity in their scenarios: Musial knew he was reaching the climax of a celebrated career, while Paciorek's—one he hoped would be just as storied—was only beginning. He had no idea that his career, like Musial's, would end on the very same day. Or that it, too, would be celebrated in a very different way, although decades later.

Musial kicked at the dirt twice, tapped the plate gently with his bat, took a couple of circular practice swings, rubbed the bat up and down with his left hand, and settled into his trademark crouch stance before fixing his gaze on the pitcher. On the mound that day was hard-throwing veteran Cincinnati Reds starter Maloney, who would toss two no-hitters and strike out two hundred or more batters four times before his career would end in 1969—the same year that Paciorek ended his own baseball run. At age forty-two, Musial's career was moments from coming to a close after more than two decades of glory and physical attrition, much of it brought on by age. He must have felt much the way Leonardo da Vinci did when the great sixteenth-century painter applied his final brushstrokes to the *Mona Lisa*. Just as da Vinci's masterpiece is among the finest works ever completed, so Musial's career was one of the most glorious to ever grace the canvas that is major-league baseball. Now, it was heading toward a close at an apposite venue: St. Louis, Missouri, home of the Cardinals, a town that Musial owned and where he would reside until his death there half a century later in 2013.

"I got to meet Stan in 1964 when one of the scouts sent me to St. Louis to work out in front of the Cardinals," said Tom Paciorek. "Stan Musial was there. I remember him distinctly asking me, 'Hey, are you Polish?' I said, 'Yes sir.' I'll never forget how gracious he was, and what a good guy! Of course, I was seventeen at the time and starstruck. Stan Musial was an all-American guy, down to earth, and a great person. I never heard a bad word about Stan Musial."

Moments after stepping in, on a 1–2 delivery from Maloney, Musial would smack a seeing-eye grounder through a narrow maw between first and second, past lunging second baseman Pete Rose, who would earn Rookie of the Year honors that year; it was twenty-two-year-old Rose who would fittingly break Musial's all-time National League record for base hits eighteen years later. Somehow this final, graceful bouncer into right seemed like a tease, as if Musial were say-ing to the rookie second baseman, whose major-league debut occurred just five months earlier, *You may become a great player someday, but at forty-two I'm still good enough to sneak one past you.*

And sneak one he did, sprinting down to first base as if age and the pounding his body had taken for so many long, arduous seasons meant nothing. To the disappointment of those in attendance that day, they would be the last sneak and sprint of Musial's illustrious career. Before the applause had fully dissipated, with the crowd's energy still being felt from foul pole to foul pole, manager Keene would summon a little-known twenty-three-year-old named Gary Kolb to pinch-run for the great Musial. Kolb, who in 1963 notched just ten RBI, was replacing a retiring legend who had nearly two hundred times that number in his career. Musial waited at first base for a couple of minutes, looking alternately down at the ground in a nervous way and up toward the dugout before focusing his sights on the steps leading to where his teammates were seated. The applause was still careening. Finally, as the standing ovation died down and fans began to once again settle back into their seats, Musial saw Kolb exit the dugout and begin to run toward first base, which for only a few more seconds would belong to him. As Kolb came nearer Musial prepared to retreat toward the St. Louis dugout for the last time. As he hesitantly broke into a stride that took him off the field, he was greeted by congratulatory teammates near the Cardinals bench. At long last, with a surge of energy and a final swing that was as picturesque and penetrable then as the first one he had taken back in 1941, as well as an implied reminder that few ballplayers, if any, were ever any better, it was over with one final and memorable single to right field. Mets announcer Nelson reported Musial's exit from baseball for WGY Radio during the Colt .45s–Mets game:

The big story of the game [in St. Louis] is that Stan Musial has played his last for the Cardinals because he left the game for pinch runner Gary Kolb, is out of action, and Musial's National League career has finished. In the first inning this afternoon Stan Musial was called out on strikes. In the fourth inning he singled to center. In the sixth inning he singled to right, scoring Flood from second, and then went out for pinch runner Gary Kolb. So, on his final day Stan Musial went 2 for 3 in National League action. And now, by courtesy of our statistician Matt Winnick, here is the career record of Stan Musial: 3,026 games, 10,973 times at bat, Musial scored 1,949 runs, he had 3,630 hits, he had 725 doubles, 177 triples, 475 home runs, 1,950 runs batted in, a lifetime batting average of .331 for Stan Musial. He was presented today with an eight-foot painting of himself by the Cardinals.

At the game that day was fourteen-year-old David Dietz, who was struck by the irony of Musial's 3,630th and final hit. Said Dietz, who appeared in a published photo standing alongside Musial's blue Cadillac before he drove away following his final game:

Stan's final at bat was in the bottom of the sixth inning and he hit a single past Pete Rose, who was then a rookie. I always thought that was a little ironic, since it was Rose who went on to break the National League hit record that Stan held. It saddened me a little when the

Cardinals pulled him out of the ballgame at that point, because my feeling was that even if the Reds were to pull ahead the Cardinals always had a chance to come back if Stan was in the lineup. He was a miracle worker, and regardless of the score Stan could turn any game around with one swing. At that point the game was close and as a boy it didn't occur to me until later that they only pulled him out so the crowd could give him one final and much-deserved standing ovation, and boy did we.[33]

Also on that day Larry Dickerson, then sixteen, had a girlfriend whose father was assigned to cover the momentous event for the *Sporting News*. As the designated equipment manager for his girlfriend's father, Dickerson got a firsthand look at Musial's routine—although his final day as a player was anything but routine. The experience, which Dickerson recounted as starting with breakfast at Musial's home, touched him deeply:

Being able to spend the game in the dugout with the great Stan Musial, being treated by all of the Cardinal players like one of them, and from time to time to be checked up on by Stan just to make sure that I was the one being treated with courtesy was a wonderful experience that I'll never forget. Throughout that memorable afternoon and evening, that was the case. It was Stan's final day playing the game he loved and he went to great lengths to make sure that I was the one having fun and feeling honored. When his final day in professional baseball had ended Stan made sure to wish me all the best and to say goodbye, and his example of true respect and gentlemanliness has never left me as I've gotten older and learned to really appreciate it. Stan was a baseball hero and superstar to many, many fans across the country and around the world, but he also was a genuinely fine person who wanted to make sure my day was as good and special as his. His kindness and respect for me as a youngster as well as the wonderful way he treated those around him expressed a true greatness that we just don't see enough of today.[34]

Simultaneously in Houston, for an unknown kid named John Paciorek, September 29, 1963, was just the beginning. Unfortunately, the day also marked the end of his own short career. In his first major league game Paciorek must have felt the same charge of excitement that Musial did over many of his nearly eleven thousand official major league at-bats, and the crowd offered him a seemingly endless round of applause that afternoon: They cheered him each time Paciorek got a base hit, drove in a run, scored a run, or made a play in the outfield—much as they had supported Musial over his career. For a single day in time Paciorek got a sense of what it might have been like to be Stan Musial, or at least to be Musial-esque— on the same day that Musial was hanging up his spikes. On that day Paciorek was better than Stan the Man: Musial collected two hits against the Reds, Paciorek got three against the Mets. Musial drove in one run, Paciorek drove in three. Musial failed to score, Paciorek scored four times. While Musial was calling it quits in St. Louis, Paciorek may have had every justification to consider himself the heir apparent. The notion didn't last long.

It did, however, last until the following morning, when newspapers across the country hailed Paciorek's impressive accomplishment while at the same time praising the great legacy that Stan Musial was leaving behind in a highly publicized departure that touched players across both leagues. "It was really special, I'll tell you that," Aspromonte said. "There was so much emphasis placed on Stan Musial [that day]."

As they read the Houston box score, which showed Paciorek's Houston Colt .45s beating the Mets 13–4, and the stories of Musial's last game and final at-bat, fans, or at least sportswriters, must have seen the irony. With every death comes a birth. Paciorek's birth had come.

Only a great and unusual performance could have competed with the retirement of a legend such as Musial, and Paciorek would have just that: a one-day career that has never been equaled, although few people in Colt Stadium or around the country would fully comprehend just how great and lasting a performance it had been until years later. It became clear when he retired from minor-league baseball in 1969 that Paciorek's one major-league game, his *force majeure*, would be his last. For the present, however, although Musial was departing, here was someone who in time might be as good as, or better than, the Polish Stanislaus. Paciorek, another Pole, simply needed a little seasoning to become as great as Musial. Maybe it wasn't such a sad day after all.

Except for one thing: the seasoning that Paciorek needed never occurred. The hits would stop, the cheering would end too quickly, and the fans would forget Paciorek sooner rather than later, much more quickly than anyone ever expected—sooner than they forgot

Musial as he stepped from the field into the dugout and disappeared from baseball. Legends linger, at least in memory, for a long, long time. In stark contrast, newcomers such as Paciorek who aren't around long enough to cut their teeth and eventually become proven veterans fade away in an instant, in the time it takes to drill a single between first and second or touch first base. That was the story line for Paciorek. He disappeared with the afternoon sun following a brief moment of baseball glory. Like Musial, and concurrently, Paciorek had played in his final major-league baseball game. He was leaving baseball forever, figuratively arm in arm with the great Stan Musial. He just didn't know it.

8

Two for Two

All I want out of life is that when I walk down the street folks will say, "There goes the greatest hitter who ever lived."
—*Ted Williams, outfielder*

This is Lindsey Nelson with Ralph Kiner and Bob Murphy at Colt Stadium in Houston, Texas. John Paciorek is up.

By the bottom of the fifth inning Houston had pulled ahead of the cellar-dwelling Mets, as most teams usually did that season, scoring five runs in the fourth to erase a 4–2 deficit. With his team up 7–4, Paciorek's emotions were running high as his third at-bat, coming on the heels of having cleanly fielded a bloop double off the bat of Hunt in the top half of the inning, lay in front of him. After walking his first time up, the muscular outfielder singled to left field in the fourth, driving in Staub and Aspromonte, who had singled consecutively to open the inning; while earning his first major-league hit Paciorek also recorded his first two RBI. He had scored two runs, made two putouts in right field, and flawlessly fielded a single in the fourth inning and a double in the fifth. He was having an unforgettable debut afternoon.

The butterflies that were dancing in his belly earlier in the game had diminished by his second time up, and with his big run-scoring single behind him Paciorek was more relaxed as he came to bat against Bauta with Aspromonte on third base following a leadoff triple to right field. There was one man out after Murrell followed Aspromonte's triple by fouling weakly to first baseman Harkness, and Paciorek, who by all rights could now call himself a true big-league ballplayer, was coming to the plate hoping to transact his third RBI of the game. His Colt .45s, who had suffered through a long and tortuous season, were now leading in the ball game, something they were unaccustomed to. Here was the rookie's chance to break the game open, or at least help his teammates build a lead that would be difficult for the lowly Mets to overcome. If he succeeded, if he got another hit, he would emerge as at least slightly heroic as the season wound to an anticlimactic close, one that most of the players on both teams had to welcome. In 1963, their second season as a major-league franchise, the Colts were not exactly a ferocious and feared run-producing machine, and neither were the last-place Mets. It was time for players to go their separate ways and rest for a couple of weeks before beginning to think about the next season. Paciorek figured to play a big role as Houston tried to climb in the standings during the 1964 campaign.

Despite his success in the game one thing caught Paciorek's attention as he walked toward the plate in the fifth inning: He would have to face a new pitcher, Bauta, the Mets' second hurler of the game. Paciorek had managed to handle the burly right hander Bearnarth all right his first two times up, drawing a walk and lifting a single, and now he was facing a pitcher who, like Bearnarth, he knew little about. One thing was obvious, however: At six foot three and two hundred pounds, Bauta was a formidable athlete and certainly a pitcher to contend with. Contend he would.

Born in Cuba and signed by the Pittsburgh Pirates in 1956, Bauta was pitching in what would be his fourth—and second to last—season. He had been traded to the Mets earlier in the season by the St. Louis Cardinals, and had not won a game since then—he was 0–0 with the Mets and 3–4 overall during what would be his most successful year as a pro. Despite his modest numbers—Bauta would finish his career with six wins and six losses over five years— it might be argued that he could at least strike batters out: In 149 innings over the course of his short big-league career Bauta would strike out eighty-nine batters, about five for every nine innings of work. Paciorek was determined he would not fall victim to the hungry right hander, whose star was fading after he put together an outstanding 1.40 earned run average in thirteen games during his second season in the big leagues, a season that had to encourage the Mets' front office. As Paciorek stepped into the batter's box, Nelson picked up the action in the announcer's booth:

> **Nelson:** And here is the pitch: breaking, low and
> away, for ball one.

Although only a first-year player, Paciorek was playing like a seasoned professional, showing veteran-like poise to avoid swinging at marginal pitches while quick to attack the good ones rather than risk looking at called strikes. It is called strikes that give a batter— and manager—fits, putting the ablest of ballplayers in a hole from which they have difficulty climbing out. Facing an 0–1, 0–2, or 1–2 count and the growing pressure that often comes with it, the result is frequently a strikeout, a blown rally, and a quick trip back to the dugout. For the most part Paciorek stayed ahead of the count, approaching each of the pitchers he faced that day the same way: aggressively—the only way he knew how to play.

"Maybe I was ultra-aggressive, because the feeling I had was that I was going to swing at every strike that I saw," Paciorek said. "I didn't care if it was a curveball or a blazing fastball, I was going to stand in there. There was no way I wasn't going to swing."

It paid off. In his book written decades later, in which he said, "Any simple-minded person can achieve baseball success,"[35] Paciorek tried to dissect his own ability to evaluate a thrown baseball in the split second after it leaves a pitcher's hand, an ability that might have helped him become an even better hitter had he developed his theory earlier and his career lasted longer than a few episodes of *Leave It to Beaver.*

"Optimal viewing of the pitched baseball is achieved when the batter's head is still and eyes remain as close as possible to a parallel level of the ball as the swing is taking place," he wrote. "Maintaining a low stance not only provides a batter with a more advantageous accommodation for the umpire's strike zone, but also affords him an optimal viewing angle from which to more accurately detect the nuances (speed and direction) of the incoming ball."[36]

The ball's nuances clearly weren't holding Paciorek back, as he'd already batted twice without making an out. His vision was on the money, too: In his final three at-bats Paciorek would look at eight balls and only two called strikes. Bauta's first pitch was a curveball outside the strike zone, and Paciorek, though perhaps surprised, wasn't fooled. With one out and Aspromonte on third base Paciorek watched the first pitch go by for a ball, and the count was 1 and 0.

> **Nelson:** Here is the [second] pitch, low for a ball. It's 2 and 0. Now time has been called, and Bauta wants to check things out with Choo-Choo Coleman. The count is 2 and 0. John Paciorek at the plate with the runner at third and one man out, the Colt .45s leading 7–4.

Behind on the count, Bauta was in a jam and called time; perhaps he stopped the game to strategize at 2–0, or to make sure he understood the signals coming from his catcher. With a runner in scoring position, Paciorek, still confident, could wait for his pitch. The gutsy Bauta would not pitch him defensively, however. Bauta was a veteran, and in a fastball situation there would be no heat here—not with a rookie at bat and at least a little pressure still residing in the young man's solar plexus. Despite Paciorek's two RBI an inning earlier, Bauta crossed him up this time:

> **Nelson:** Here's the pitch, in for a called strike, a breaking ball, it's 2 and 1. One man out and a runner at third, we're in the bottom half of the fifth inning. Mets still have the infield in.

A curveball with the pitcher behind on the count, behind in the game, and a runner on third base with the infield drawn in was a risky move. Although Bauta wasn't the flamethrower that some of his contemporaries were, he was a pro and was having a fair year, considering that he was pitching for his third team in what had to be a long and challenging season. Would he push his luck and come back with another curveball? History doesn't reveal what pitch he threw next, just that it was within reach and that Paciorek was waiting for it. It would be the last pitch that Bauta would ever serve the young rookie during the brief time that their "careers" intersected. Although Bauta would return the following spring he would pitch just ten more innings in a final season of baseball, the product of eight appearances—all of them for the Mets. Bauta would retire with a lifetime earned run average of 4.35, respectable for a part-time (and well-traveled!) pitcher even by today's standards.

> **Nelson:** Bauta looks for his sign, up and sets. Here's the 2–1 pitch: It's swung on and looped into left field for a base hit, a handle hit but it's gonna score a run. Bob Aspromonte jogs across the plate—Paciorek holds with his second major-league base hit, his third run batted in. This is his first major-league game, he's having a big day—he's 2 for 2 and a walk, has scored two runs, driven in three.

Little did Bauta know that his fourth pitch to Paciorek would catapult him onto the pages of baseball history as one of three pitchers who would give up hits to the gritty teen in that history-making performance.

"The announcer thought he jammed me, which he probably did. It sounded like I muscled it over the shortstop's head between second and third."

Despite allowing the single and the inauspicious place in baseball lore that the base hit earned him, Bauta had no memory of Paciorek when reached by telephone at his Florida home.

"I'm sorry, I don't remember," he said. "It's been so long. I'm sorry."

After two hits by the rookie phenomenon, the broadcast team was beginning to take notice, with Nelson mentioning twice in one breath that Paciorek had collected his second hit and that he now had three RBI and two runs scored. Paciorek had moved beyond the 1-for-1 performance that most successful one-game wonders enjoyed and was now in elite territory, especially with his collection of RBI and runs scored added to his totals. Only a handful of players went 2 for 2 in their only major-league game, and Paciorek would have two more chances to improve on that. Improve he would.

After he walked the rookie catcher Bateman, the Mets replaced the ineffective Bauta with relief pitcher Tracy Stallard, who had gained notoriety in 1961 by serving up Yankee slugger Roger Maris's record-breaking sixty-first home run on the final day of the season. After working only one and a third innings, Bauta was gone, headed for the showers. His statistics that day were less than impressive: four hits and three runs allowed (all of them earned), one walk, and a strikeout. And no memory of the feisty Paciorek, whose second hit set the table for the pitcher's early trip to the Colt Stadium lockers and a head start on his final season in baseball.

With his team leading 8–4 and a full count on Bateman, Paciorek broke for second on a pitch that was hit foul. After fouling off several more pitches Bateman walked, sending Paciorek cruising down to second. Bauta was relieved by Stallard, bringing up shortstop Bob Lillis, who replaced Vaughan to effectively end his career as well.

Nelson: Swing and a ground ball off the glove of

Hickman and out into left field. Rounding third and coming home is Paciorek, the throw to the plate—he goes in standing up.

With that run the numbers were piling up for Paciorek, as they would for the Colts all day long: two hits, three RBI, three runs scored, two putouts, and clean pickups of a single and a bloop double for the young outfielder, who was gaining experience with every inning. His Colt .45s were showing good productivity, too. They would hit through the batting order for the second consecutive inning, scoring four more runs to go ahead 11–4. Paciorek, with his team pulling away thanks largely to his own exploits, was having the time of his life, and things couldn't get much better. Or, he must have wondered, could they? Within the next few innings Paciorek would have his fourth chance at the plate. Little did he know that a base hit could set the stage for him to complete the most remarkable one-game career that any player had ever experienced—and perhaps *would* ever. All he had to do was hit the ball where nobody was, something he was proving quite adept at. Could anyone ever get him out?

9

Hubbs of the Cubs

I live and die with the Chicago Cubs.
—Sara Paretsky, author

Chicago Cubs announcer Jack Brickhouse, September 5, 1962: The 2–1 pitch to Johnny Edwards: fastball hit on the ground to Kenny Hubbs. Here it is, a record breaker—he throws him out, and that's number 415 for Hubbs, which breaks the [major-league] record. He just threw Johnny Edwards out to retire the side, and it's the 415th consecutive chance for Hubbs without an error. [Umpire] Dusty Boggess gives him the baseball and that'll go in a very treasured place. Hubbs comes out and accepts the ball from Boggess and tips his cap, acknowledging the cheers of fans.

With all of the subtle disadvantages he had to overcome relative to other ballplayers of his era, Kenneth Douglas Hubbs might have failed in his quest to become an outstanding major-league baseball player, or at least achieved it more slowly than he did. Even mediocrity would have been a fair outcome, considering he came from nowhere special, played high school ball for no one of note, and was drafted by a perennial loser—the Cubs. His premature death percolated in what had become a truly bad century for the Cubs.

Hubbs was born in Riverside, California— hardly a font of baseball prowess. He attended Colton High School, which opened to students in 1896 as the first high school in the Colton Unified School District and was not known as a prep baseball powerhouse. He did not attend college as many players of his era did, particularly those who wished to gain some experience above and beyond the high school level as well as exposure to major-league scouts. Instead, he went straight to the minor leagues for a two-year stint after signing with the Chicago Cubs, a team that had not won a World Series (and still hasn't) since back-to-back championships in 1907 and 1908. Still, in just two full seasons as a major leaguer Hubbs left an indelible mark, earning National League Rookie of the Year honors in 1962, largely due to his fine fielding (although in those two seasons combined he also managed to hit fourteen home runs and drive in ninety-eight runs), which earned him a Gold Glove award. He was the first rookie to achieve that distinction for fielding excellence, an honor that was well deserved. And when Hubbs was killed in an airplane crash on February 15, 1963, with the aircraft he was piloting plunging onto a frozen lake near Provo, Utah, his name became forever linked with those of John Paciorek, Stan Musial and Jim Umbricht: Like theirs, Hubbs's final game occurred on September 29, 1963. Newspapers large and small around the country, like the *Spartanburg Herald-Journal* in South Carolina, announced it to readers, who reacted with stunned disbelief:

Ken Hubbs, 22, star second baseman for the Chicago Cubs, and a friend were found dead Saturday in the wreckage of a light plane that crashed on a frozen lake near Provo [Utah].

The death of the fielding great ended a bright career highlighted by his selection as the National League's Rookie of the Year in 1962.

Hubbs and his companion, Dennis Doyle, 22, left [Provo] in Hubbs' single-engine plane Thursday morning for their homes in Colton, Calif.; they got only about five miles. The wreckage of the aircraft was sighted on the ice of Utah Lake, just south of Provo, late Saturday morning.[37]

That Hubbs, both handsome and skilled, should perish in such a tragic way and at such a young age, after accomplishing so much in such a short period of time, is a tragedy in itself. That generations of baseball fans, in particular Cubs die-hards whose hopes for a championship were renewed when the slender second sacker came along, were not able to see him reach his potential as an infielder, whatever that might have been, is almost as tragic. Because Hubbs, as much in hindsight as he was when he played, is considered one of the greatest-fielding second basemen ever to play the game. He was so good that his outstanding offensive statistics during his rookie season often took a backseat to his fielding stats, which included just 15 errors in 867 chances and a .983 fielding percentage.

Perhaps the late sports columnist Jim Murray described him best in a column that ran in the *Los Angeles Times* shortly after Hubbs died: "Kenneth Douglass Hubbs was more than just another baseball player," he wrote. "He was the kind of athlete all games need. A devout Mormon, a cheerful leader, a picture-book player, blond-haired, healthy, generous with his time for young boys; he was the kind of youth in short supply in these selfish times."[38]

Teammate Ron Santo, a Hubbs pallbearer who passed away in 2010, had difficulty understanding the sudden and tragic demise of his young friend and roommate.

"Ken and I were both religious," he said in an interview shortly after Hubbs's death. "We were always joking—trying to convert each other. I'm a Catholic, he was a Mormon. But after he died I had to see a priest. I couldn't understand it. I mean, he loved life. He was a great human being. This was a kid who didn't even smoke or drink. Why him?"[39]

The tombstone that graces Hubbs's grave summed up his life through the lens of his family's, friends', and fans' love even better than any newspaper column could, concurring with Murray in more succinct and touching fashion. It reads, simply, "Our Ken—Kenneth D. Hubbs, Dec. 23, 1941–Feb. 13, 1964."

Born in California's Inland Empire roughly fifty-five miles east of Los Angeles in a community situated near the Santa Ana River—hence the name of his hometown Riverside—Hubbs wasted little time achieving baseball stardom as a youth, playing in the 1954 Little League World Series in Williamsport, Pennsylvania, as a member of the Colton Lions team that lost to Schenectady, New York, 5–3; he played shortstop and went 2 for 4 with an RBI and two runs scored in that final game, which may have marked his coming out to the baseball world he someday would captivate. Opposing him on the winning team were two future major leaguers, Jim Barbieri, who broke in with the Dodgers in 1966, and Bill Connors, who briefly played for the Cubs that same year. Despite playing only two full seasons and part of a third, Hubbs would play in more games than Barbieri and Connors combined did in their careers and enjoy considerably more success and even fame.

Not that fame was what he sought, although it seemed to come with the territory. After losing in the Little League World Series, Hubbs's fate was sealed when the runner-up Colton squad took the players and their families to a Cubs game at Wrigley Field. His idol at the time was Mr. Cub, Ernie Banks, who only a decade later would help carry the casket at his funeral.

Five years following his Little League success Hubbs graduated from Colton High, where he played baseball, basketball, and football and was elected student body president. Despite his prowess in the other sports—he was named a high school all-American in basket-ball and football—baseball was his first love, and he signed with the Cubs in 1959 as an amateur free agent. He played rookie ball for Morristown of the Appalachian League and Fort Worth of the American Association later that same year. The following season, 1960, found him playing single-A and double-A ball in San Antonio of the Texas League and Lancaster of the Eastern League, followed by Wenatchee of the Northwest League, the Cubs' Class B team, in 1961. Throughout his brief minor-league career Hubbs played shortstop, just as he did in Little League. His streak of playing short would end quietly during the 1961 season when the Cubs moved him to second base for good.

Hubbs debuted for the Cubs on September 10, 1961, playing second, a position he eventually would squeeze veteran Don Zim-mer out of in 1962. In ten games during the '61 campaign he hit just .179 with a double, a triple, a home run, and two RBI. Perhaps due to his fielding prowess—in twenty-eight chances he had thirteen putouts, fifteen assists, and zero errors for a perfect 1.000 fielding percentage—the Cubs had high hopes, and in 1962 he played in all but two games. During the long season he hit twenty-four doubles, nine triples, and five home runs; however, he also led the league in strikeouts while hitting into more double plays than any other player. When the dust had cleared he was a landslide winner over Donn Clendenon of the Pittsburgh Pirates to win Rookie of the Year honors.

With his successful rookie year behind him, Hubbs started the 1963 season with even higher expectations, and he played in 154 games. With the pressure of his breakout rookie season diminished, his statistics also ebbed, in some ways significantly. Hubbs's at-bat total dropped from 661 to 556, largely because he played in fewer games. The number of hits he collected also declined sharply from 172 to 133, and he slugged nineteen doubles compared with twenty-four and three triples compared with nine. Although Hubbs had three more home runs during his sophomore season—eight in all—his RBI total also dipped slightly, from forty-nine in 1962 to forty-seven in 1963. Perhaps most dramatic was the drop in his batting average, from .260 down to .235.

As Hubbs's offensive numbers dwindled so did his defensive statistics. In 853 chances in the field he had seven more errors (twenty-two) than he had in all of 1962, and his fielding percentage dropped from .983 to .974. He also turned seven fewer double plays than he had the previous season. These were not at all the numbers that management had hoped for following his impressive Rookie of the Year season.

In his final game at the end of the 1963 season, while Musial was collecting two hits and Paciorek three in what also would also be their final major-league games, Hubbs finished with a whimper. Batting fifth in the lineup behind cleanup hitter Santo, who would continue on to become a formidable home run hitter over the course of an impressive career, Hubbs failed to get a hit or drive in a run in a 2–0 loss to the Milwaukee Braves. His performance was perhaps understandable: In that game forty-two-year-old pitching legend Warren Spahn threw a complete-game, four-hit shutout to notch his twenty-third win of the season. The veteran Spahn would not win that many games total over the final four years of his career.

Although Hubbs was disappointed, there were some bright spots in his final season. He struck out less, only 93 times compared with 129 the previous year—he would not lead the league in that unenviable category for the second consecutive season. He also walked more, demonstrating a keen eye and the patience required to wait for his pitch. And his stolen base total was more than twice what it was in 1962. Clearly, there were things to be hopeful about in 1964.

But for Hubbs the 1964 season would never arrive—ironically, it took an airplane to bring him back down to earth.

Throughout the years the different modes of transportation that professional baseball teams used to travel from one city to another changed with the times and included buses, trains, propeller-driven aircraft, and jet planes. When the National League was established in 1876, trains were the only vehicle logically capable of transporting large numbers of players between towns that were situated hundreds of miles apart. At that time there were no automobiles, let alone paved highways, and few acceptable dirt roads. Besides—traveling over dirt roads for hundreds of miles would not have been practical, especially if teams wanted their players to arrive at destinations without the bumps and bruises that could marginalize their play. Although stagecoaches were still in use when major-league baseball began, they were limited as to how many passengers they could carry, how fast they could go, and how many miles they could reasonably cover in twenty-four hours under the best of circumstances.

By the turn of the twentieth century it still took up to a full day for teams traveling by train to pass from one baseball city to another. However, that began to change with the advent of the automobile in the early 1900s and the Wright brothers' first successful flight in 1903. As paved roads and airports began to proliferate, it wouldn't be too many years before buses and airplanes became the preferred methods of transportation for major- and minor-league baseball teams, which by then were dotting the country.

In 1882 the average distance between major-league ballparks was 430 miles, and by 1955 it was 469 miles. By 1962, when travel by jet was gaining wide acceptance, the average distance had more than doubled in eighty years, up to 898 miles. And by 1969, when travel by jetliner was firmly established in major-league baseball, the average distance between ballparks was a whopping 1,158 miles—more than it was in 2005 (1,155 miles).[40] Jet travel was the logical means of bridging the distance gap.

On June 8, 1934, the Cincinnati Reds flew their players to Chicago for a series against, perhaps ironically, the Chicago Cubs; it marked the first time air travel had been used in major-league baseball. By the late 1930s more and more major-league teams were similarly finding airplane travel to their liking. In 1946, the New York Yankees carried air travel a step further, contracting for a Douglas Aircraft DC-4 to carry its players to various cities throughout the 154-game season.[41]

The handwriting was on the wall: Air transportation for professional baseball teams was here to stay.[42]

Still, even in an era of high-speed transportation minor leaguers, especially those at the rookie, single-A, and double-A levels, continued to travel by bus, propagating a term used by players in what has long been known as the bush leagues.

"I played eight seasons in the 'bus leagues' and traveling by bus is not only cost-effective for the team but it's practical, since the cities you travel to are not that far from one another—a few hundred miles at most," said Neil Rasmussen, a first-round draft pick for Houston who played single-A and double-A ball in the Houston and Milwaukee organizations. "It's all part of the training. A five-hour bus ride is no different than a five-hour plane flight—you still have to play baseball when you get to your destination.

"Even major-league teams ride buses to cities that are nearby, as well as from airports to hotels, from hotels to the ballpark, then back to the airport when a series is completed. Riding a bus is part of life for a ballplayer."

Although jet travel came along in the 1950s, as 1963 rolled around—when Hubbs was in his third year with the Cubs—prop-driven aircraft were still very much in use. Compared with modern jetliners those planes were jerky and unpredictable, often resulting in "white-knuckle" flying. Hubbs, like many players of both his era and now, was not a fan of bumpy flying. He apparently let others know it, including roommate and future pallbearer Santo.

At some point Hubbs decided to take flying lessons in a likely effort to overcome his fear. He probably reasoned that the knowledge he would gain might help diminish his aversion to air travel. With the dozens of flights the team took each year, and the stress it likely caused him each time a plane took off and landed, the prospect of better understanding that which he feared—flying—had to be appealing.

There is no indication the Cubs officially objected to his flying lessons, even after the plane went down with Hubbs at the controls. "We can't regulate everything the players do in the winter," Cubs athletic director Bob Whitlow, a retired air force colonel, said after the crash. He added, however, "It's just a shock. It's just too tragic to believe."[43]

Hubbs received his pilot's license in January 1964, some time after purchasing a Cessna 72 aircraft. He wasted little time taking advantage of his newfound freedom of the skies, flying from Colton to Provo, Utah, the following month with his best friend and high school chum, Doyle. There to participate in a basketball clinic sponsored by Brigham Young University and the Church of Jesus Christ of Latter-Day Saints, the two had made the flight without incident. However, departing in foul weather for the return trip to Morrow Field near Colton, the plane apparently encountered a storm shortly after leaving Provo Airport and went down, breaking apart on icy Provo Lake, partially submerging and killing both men instantly. The plane was located the next day, February 16, 1964, following a three-state search that was initiated after Hubbs's father reported that his son's plane had failed to arrive in Colton as expected.

It was later revealed that at the time of the crash Hubbs had only seventy-one hours of training, a shortcoming that may have indirectly cost him his life. The Civil Aeronautics Board determined that the crash was caused by pilot error—specifically, Hubbs was not rated for instrument flying and ventured into an area where weather was poor, causing him to lose control of the aircraft. [44] Hubbs had lost his life; the city of Colton, whose Little League was renamed the Ken Hubbs Memorial Little League, had lost its favorite son; and the Cubs had lost its star of the future.

The Cubs decided to go with thirty-year-old Joey Amalfitano at second base in 1964. He hit a meager .241 with four home runs and twenty-seven RBI in a hundred games. Amalfitano also made more errors—seventeen—in roughly half as many chances—472—as Hubbs had during his entire Rookie of the Year season.

While the Cubs rightfully did not retire Hubbs's uniform number 16 following his untimely death, they did not assign it to another player for several more years—until Roger Metzger wore it during the 1970 season, batting .000 with two at-bats and reminding everyone that a key piece of the Cubs puzzle was still sorely missing. Since then, nearly two dozen players have worn number 16. They include Garry Jestadt (1971), Gene Hiser (1971–72), Whitey Lockman (1972–74), Rob Sperring (1974–76), Steve Ontiveros (1977–80), Bill Hayes (1980–81), Steve Lake (1983–86), Terry Francona (1986), Paul Noce (1987), Greg Smith (1989–90), Jose Vizcaino (1991–93), Anthony Young (1994–95), Dave Magadan (1996), Jeff Reed (1999–2000), Delino Deshields (2001–02), Sonny Jackson (2003), Aramis Ramirez (2003–11), Joe Mather (2012), and Jeff Beliveau (2012)[45]—most of them unheralded. Only Ontiveros, Lake, and Ramirez wore it longer than Hubbs had, with Ramirez wearing it the longest of any of those players: nine years. Although half a century has passed since Hubbs last wore uniform number 16, in the minds of Cubs fans he remains the most prominent person to wear that number since Hall of Famer Jimmie Foxx last did so during the 1942 season. The comparison between the two players —Foxx was a three-time Most Valuable Player with the Philadelphia

Athletics and Boston Red Sox before retiring in 1945—is not lost. Foxx, a slick-fielding first baseman/third baseman, represented all that Hubbs might have become—except for the venerable Foxx's propensity to hit home runs—had he lived to play out his promising career. Coincidentally, the final All-Star game appearance for Foxx occurred in 1941—the year that Hubbs was born.

In its article "Best of the Cubs by Uniform Number,"[46] the *Chicago Tribune* proclaimed Ramirez the best of all who wore number 16 for any length of time (Foxx wore it for just one season). However, it added a caveat, calling Hubbs "as smooth a second baseman as you'll ever see. That we only got to see him two years is one of Chicago baseball's great tragedies." More than half a century later, Cubs fans still need no reminder of that.

Lou Boudreau, Hall of Fame pitcher, former Most Valuable Player, and a Cubs radio announcer at the time of Hubbs's death, identified the player's potential in the simplest of terms: "At the time he died, I felt he was on his way to a Hall of Fame career."[47]

10

Good as a Hit

The only thing wrong with the Mets is that we don't play them enough.
—George Kirksey, executive, Houston Colt .45s and Houston Astros

Lindsey Nelson: Here's a young man, John Paciorek, making his major-league debut today, and he walked, singled to drive in two runs, singled to drive in one run, he has scored three himself.

The essence of Paciorek's offensive performance was not lost on Nelson, nor should it have been. The veteran announcer, who began his broadcast career fifteen seasons earlier, in 1948, was a true pro. He knew the game of baseball inside out, was astute to its many intricacies, and to fill nine innings of play-by-play he, Kiner, and Murphy had to be alert to everything—including a rookie player's potentially historic debut. That's what was happening in the person of John Paciorek, and Nelson knew it.

Born in 1919 in Pulaski, Tennessee, Nelson began broadcasting after teaching English, working as a reporter for two Knoxville news-papers, and serving as a war correspondent during World War II. After working for the Liberty Broadcasting System, doing baseball game re-creations much like Ronald Reagan had done at the beginning of his own broadcast career, Nelson also worked as an administrator with NBC Sports, a position that gave him entrée to begin broadcasting the network's baseball games with Leo Durocher beginning in 1957, a run that ended in 1961. During his long career with NBC he also broadcast National Basketball Association games, National Football League games, professional tennis and golf, and National Collegiate Athletic Association football games alongside the Galloping Ghost, professional football Hall of Famer Red Grange. During his illustrious career Nelson called two World Series, twenty-six Cotton Bowl games, four Rose Bowl games, and one major-league All-Star game.

Although capable of announcing any sport with great skill, it was baseball that provided Nelson with a stage where his abilities truly shone. Like Kiner and Murphy, the erudite announcer joined the Mets' broadcast team in 1962, the team's first season as a major-league franchise, and he spent seventeen seasons with the club, working alongside Kiner and Murphy during that entire period; he reportedly left because the club was so consistently awful, the 1969 and 1973 world championship teams notwithstanding.[48]

Nelson: Grover Powell with the pitch: Paciorek swings and misses, he's a right-hand batter.

Paciorek began his penultimate at bat with a swinging strike, at once putting him behind on the count. He had also swung at a first pitch in the second inning when he fouled off the opening delivery from Bearnarth, but eventually earned a walk from the twenty-two-year-old. Throughout the game Paciorek was eager to hit the ball. "My strategy that day was simple: I was going to stand in there and try to get every ounce of power I could swing with," he said. "I didn't care if I got hit by the pitch. It worked okay, except for the fact that my mechanics were so horrible."

As he waited for the next delivery, coming from the third pitcher he had faced that day, Paciorek wondered about the man on the mound. Powell, appearing in his twentieth game, was also a rookie, and his statistics that season had been confounding: forty-nine innings pitched with thirty-nine strikeouts and thirty-two walks—roughly seven strikeouts and six walks every nine innings pitched. With one out and the bases empty Paciorek stared out at Powell and waited for the lefty to come back at him.

Nelson: Powell's fastball is low, it's 1–1.

With the count even Paciorek could relax a little as he waited for a pitch that he could drive. If it didn't come and Powell managed to pop the corner of the plate, or perhaps come in at the knees or the letters for a second strike, he would still have another shot or two at pounding the baseball for his third base hit of the game, making him an unlikely hero at 3 for 3. Already he had surpassed the success that Modesto teammate Lee Roy Hyman might have expected of him. Hyman remembered Paciorek as a modest hitter.

"I knew he got called up—he was a big, strong guy, but I'd never have thought they would call him up," said Hyman. "It seems like I remember him having some back trouble.

"I remember him being strong and not hitting too well."

Nelson: That pitch is high.

At 2 and 1 Paciorek had moved ahead on the count, giving him a distinct advantage as he waited for Powell to throw again. Another ball would make the count 3 and 1 and Powell would have to deliver a strike—an enviable position for any batter: When a pitcher is forced to throw a strike, often a fastball, the batter gains leverage. As Powell set to throw, Paciorek went into his familiar stance.

Nelson: Here's a pitch low, it's 3 and 1.

Paciorek, on the verge of receiving his second walk of the game, was in the driver's seat. He could watch another pitch go by, even a strike, and still force another good pitch from his counterpart on the mound. Home run hitters such as Paciorek relish a 3-and-1 count, because it gives them two chances to hit a pitch they can drive over the fence. As a slugging threat, Paciorek understood the situation he was in. He knew Powell would have to throw a strike or suffer the consequences of another possible earned-run-average-inflating rally.

> **Nelson:** Here's a pitch swung on and it is in the air, in foul territory to the right side. [Catcher Chris] Canizzaro goes as far as he can go and the wind helps this one into the stands and out of play.

The count was now full and Paciorek was forcing the young

pitcher to come back again with a pitch down the middle. Although "I never wanted two strikes on me," this situation was different. Powell had thrown a strike at 3–1, and the odds were against an inexperienced pitcher like he was coming across with a second consecutive strike on a three-ball count. Paciorek was still in the position of either receiving a pitch he could hit or letting ball four go by. There was one proviso: "I knew these were big leaguers, and I knew big leaguers threw strikes. The only time a pitcher almost hit someone was when he did it deliberately."

Paciorek didn't know it then, but Powell would never pitch in another ball game, and at some level there had to be pressure on the twenty-two-year-old Sayre, Pennsylvania, native, who may have sensed his own career was winding down. At the end of the day both Paciorek and Powell would slip into more private lives—more so Powell, who would die from leukemia in 1985 at the age of forty-four, than the man he was facing at the plate. He had to throw a strike on the next pitch.

> **Nelson:** Right here the Colt .45s are leading the Mets by a score of 11–4 on the final day of the season. Grover Powell waiting until Chris Canizzaro is set behind the plate. And the payoff pitch: low and he walked him. Paciorek goes to first.

Powell had lost him. After starting out ahead of the batter he threw three straight balls, went all the way at 3 and 2, then walked him. Paciorek was pleased. He had come to bat four times, reaching base on each occasion, and the possibility that he would bat again was strong. Still, the sixth inning was not over: the fleet-footed rookie had some more base running to do.

With Paciorek on first and one out Powell threw a wild pitch, enabling Paciorek to scramble down to second base. Bateman then grounded to third with Paciorek holding at second, bringing up the shortstop Lillis.

Nelson: Powell checks and deals: Pitch is swung on, looped into center field for a base hit, Paciorek rounds third, he's coming home. The Colt .45s, with 12 runs in this game, have reached their season high—they lead 12–4.

Through six innings Paciorek's Colt .45s had scored a dozen runs, and seven of them were due to their newfound star's sterling play—his hitting and base running. He had singled twice, driven in three runs, and scored four more. With three innings left to play the excitement was building, and Paciorek was enjoying every minute of it. From here on out everything else would be icing on the cake. Or would his final at-bat, with the Colts holding a commanding lead, still mean something? It would to Paciorek, and it ultimately would have a bearing on baseball history.

11

Big Jim

It ain't over till it's over.
—Yogi Berra, catcher

In perhaps his most colloquial Yogi-ism, the New York Yankees' eccentric catcher spoke volumes when he talked about a ball game being over. When it's over, it's over. Unfortunately, the last guy to know is often the person who should know first. For "Big Jim" Umbricht, a six-foot-four, 215-pound relief pitcher with the floundering Houston Colts, it was over on September 29, 1963: game, season, career, and soon life itself. Unlike Stan Musial, who knew unequivocally his career was over on that very same afternoon and who chose to walk away with few regrets, and Paciorek, whose chronic back pain gave him reason to fear that his own career might be in jeopardy, Umbricht probably wasn't certain it was time to hang up his spikes until the metastatic melanoma that had infiltrated his body had progressed to the point of causing his muscular frame to degenerate. Paradoxically, Ken Hubbs was the only player of the four whose careers would end on that day who truly believed without a doubt that he would return to play for his team in 1964. However, personal assurance and the certainty of a young man in the prime of athleticism mean nothing when a snowstorm and a light plane with a rookie pilot at the controls go head-to-head high above a frozen Utah lake. Just weeks after Hubbs's untimely death Umbricht also would lose his life.

The Associated Press reported Umbricht's death in an article that appeared in the *New York Times* on April 8, 1964. It didn't even note the specific cause of his death, calling it, generally, "cancer." There are many forms of the disease, each of them treated differently, and Umbricht's was an ominous and often deadly version: melanoma, which each year kills more than nine thousand Americans.[49] Wrote the AP:

(AP)—Jim Umbricht, Houston Colt right-handed relief pitcher, died today of cancer. He was 33 years old.

Despite a six-hour operation on March 7, 1963, he was in uniform on opening day last season and before the season ended he compiled a 4–3 record in 76 innings as a relief pitcher. He gave up 52 hits, struck out 48 batters, allowed 21 walks and had a 2.61 earned run average.

The Colts purchased Umbricht from the Pittsburgh Pirates for $50,000 in the National League player pool in 1961. In Umbricht's first year in the majors, 1962, he had a 4–0 record. His five-year record at Pittsburgh and Houston was 194 innings in 88 games for a 9–5 record and a 3.06 earned run average.

The athlete was a graduate of the University of Georgia, where he played both baseball and basketball. In 1951 he was named All-Southeastern Conference shortstop.[50]

It had been thirteen months since Umbricht was diagnosed with melanoma in March 1963—right about spring training time. The cancer first became obvious to him during a golf outing as a lump on his right thigh and eventually, almost methodically, it overcame him. He underwent surgery to remove the tumor on March 7, 1963,[51] and gamely suited up for opening day three weeks later. For Umbricht, his family, the Colts, and their fans, things looked hopeful, at least on the surface. However, as it turned out there was little realistic reason for long-term optimism. Umbricht's cancer reappeared in his chest during the 1963 season and eventually cut him down just weeks after he was honored as the league's most courageous player for his long fight against cancer; his body was cremated and his ashes scattered over the Astrodome construction site. The domed stadium, it seemed, would forever serve as a massive, and fitting, headstone for a man whose strength and courage were larger than life—and death.

Umbricht's passing right before opening day 1964, and less than two months before Hubbs would die prematurely, prompted the Colts to wear black armbands during the entire season.[52] Perhaps in gratitude for his positive attitude, fighting spirit, unwavering commitment to a long-struggling team, and genuine congeniality toward everyone he came in contact with, the Colt .45s announced on the same day that they would retire his uniform number. As expected, there were quiet rumblings. Based upon Umbricht's athletic ability alone, some probably wondered whether he deserved to have his number 32 retired—the first number the Houston organization would ever remove from service and one of nine retired by the franchise since the Colts first took the field in 1962.[53] From a purely statistical standpoint, he probably didn't deserve the honor. Today Umbricht may be the least known major-league ballplayer to have had his number retired by a team.

"It was something special, and the reason for that was not so much what he accomplished on the field," said Aspromonte, proud winner of the Jim Umbricht Award as the team's most valuable player in 1964 and a close friend of the pitcher. "It was [what he did] off the field, and also—he went through a lot in the last year. We were all conscious of that, more so than getting a base hit." Retiring Umbricht's number, he said, "was a lot different" than retiring the numbers of other players, most of whom were largely honored for their on-field accomplishments.

Outside of Houston, where he ended his career, and Pittsburgh, where he pitched during the shaky first three years of what would be a short career, few people knew much about the lanky right-hander. In all, he pitched for just five seasons, the first two of them inglorious ones: 1959, 0–0 with a 6.43 earned run average in seven innings pitched for the Pittsburgh Pirates. And 1960, 1–2 with a 5.09 ERA in forty and two-thirds innings pitched, again for the Pirates.

After that things improved measurably. In 1961, his final season as a mostly part-time player for the Pirates, Umbricht was 0–0 with a 2.70 ERA in three and a third innings. He then was sent to Houston, an expansion club that gave him ample opportunity to gain some experience while at the same time prove himself as a major-league-caliber pitcher. To players, that was the positive side of expansion baseball in the early 1960s: Those who otherwise might not have an opportunity to make the big leagues found an extra hundred positions to fill—on the twenty-five-man rosters of the 1961 American League expansion Los Angeles Angels and Washington Senators and the National League Mets and Colts. Umbricht made the most of his opportunity. In 1962 he went 4–0 with a 2.01 ERA in sixty-seven innings pitched, and in 1963 he had nearly as good a season, going 4–3 with a 2.61 ERA in seventy-six innings. In just two seasons he had gone from being a bit player to one of the National League's top relievers. With his workload increasing each of the first two seasons with Houston, Umbricht's stock was clearly on the rise.

Then came the crash, a devastating one that must have taken nearly everyone in the Colt organization by surprise, especially since Umbricht had kept his cancer recurrence quiet. His last victory, although at the time he earned it he had no idea he would never pitch again, came during Paciorek's debut with Houston. Umbricht relieved rookie starter Zachary in the fourth inning just in time for his teammates to erase a 4–2 Mets lead and score five runs to go ahead. Houston would not trail in the game after that rally, and Umbricht would pick up the win. His line for that day: in two-thirds of an inning pitched he gave up one hit and struck out one. He finished his career with a 9–5 record and a 3.06 ERA.

"He had a lot more productive years ahead of him, especially with the new Colt franchise," Aspromonte said. "It would've been a great opportunity for him to continue on."

It was on April 9, 1964, when owner Hofheinz announced that the Colts would retire Umbricht's number. Later, there would be whisperings that perhaps number 32 should have remained in circulation, that Umbricht's career lacked the plenitude, including the years and statistics, to warrant his jersey being framed and hung on a wall someplace within the confines of Colt Stadium. In his autobiography, teammate Wynn, whose number was retired by the organization in 2005, raised the issue of disparity involving the club's retirement of Umbricht's number and its failure to retire Walt Bond's number after he died: "If the Houston club believed that it was fitting and proper to retire Jim Umbricht's uniform number 32 in his honor, which they did, why couldn't they have done the same for Walt Bond and retired his number too?" he wondered. "Bond even played more games as a Colt .45."[54]

He added a caveat: "Both Umbricht and Bond were fine human beings who cared about others and died way too young for any of us to understand God's plan for each."[55]

There was a difference between Bond, a black man who played outfield/first base for six seasons, and the five-year veteran Umbricht, who was white. Bond, who died from leukemia in 1967 at the age of twenty-nine,[56] finished his career in Minnesota with a different team and in a different league. Clearly, at the end of their lives, Houston's affection for a man who had ended his playing days with the team—a team whose existence he helped usher in and that ultimately he lived and died with—was greater than it was for an athlete who was playing his heart out for another franchise.

In allowing Umbricht's ashes to be scattered where the iconic Astrodome would soon be built, Houston was sending a message: The team wanted him to be forever integrated into the club infrastructure. The Colts wanted the pride of Umbricht's hometown Chicago, his college town, Athens, Georgia, and now Houston to be remembered for all eternity as a Colt, a founding son, as did Umbricht's brother, Ed, who flew over the site in a small plane to scatter the ashes in a city—Houston—he still calls home.

"I was his brother and I've got nothing but good things to say about Jim," Umbricht said. "He was a fabulous human being, a magnet for children. When he entered a room children flocked to him."

Asked about Houston's decision to retire his brother's uniform number following his death, Umbricht admitted it was an unusual gesture and said it probably was due to Jim's kindness toward others, especially children, and because of his personal magnetism. Hofheinz's respect for Umbricht brought about the unusual move, he said, one that was never redacted as other teams have done after retiring a number under the shadow of emotion or other considerations.

"The team did it because of the type of guy he was, the owner did it on his own volition," Ed said. "He said Jim was such a good person that he was going to retire his number."

Born in Chicago, Illinois, on September 17, 1930, Umbricht was raised in Georgia and attended the University of Georgia–Athens, where he captained the Bulldog basketball team and became an all-conference shortstop on the baseball team. He broke in with the Milwaukee Braves organization in 1953,[57] playing for Waycross in the Georgia–Florida League and parts of three more seasons with Baton Rouge, Topeka, and Atlanta (he spent 1954 and 1955 in the service). Milwaukee traded him to the Pittsburgh Pirates in 1959, and he played most of that year with the team's triple-A Salt Lake City affiliate, the Bees, before making his major-league debut on September 26, 1959, as the season was coming to a close.

Under the growing weight of news media predictions that he would be a rookie sensation in 1960 Umbricht struggled early on and instead was optioned back to Salt Lake City, where he remained until the season was nearly over. Called back up toward the end of the Pirates' pennant-winning season, Umbricht did not play in the World Series against the Yankees, which Pittsburgh won, 4–3, on Bill Mazeroski's dramatic ninth-inning home run in the seventh and final game.

Umbricht remained in the minor leagues for most of the 1961 season before Houston bought him for $50,000 in the National League player pool, breathing new life into his stalled career. His 1963 Topps baseball card may have best described the high hopes that Houston and the fans had for him during what would turn out to be his final season with the club. The card read, prophetically: "The Colts are counting on Jim to become their bullpen ace."[58]

That prediction arguably came to pass. In the two seasons Umbricht played for Houston his ERA averaged less than 2.50, outstanding by any gauge either then or now. After those two seasons the pitcher appeared to be headed toward a successful career in the major leagues.

Then came the malignant melanoma, which struck like lightning and nibbled away at Umbricht's once-robust health the following year until he had no choice but to call it quits. It couldn't have been an easy decision to leave the game he loved, one that promised him long-term success as he gained major-league footing and matured into an experienced big-league pitcher. However, as his illness progressed and overtook his body, it became clear that Umbricht was through.

Perhaps his brother articulated it best when asked how great a career the cancer may have short-circuited when it claimed the life of his only sibling, whose achievements and persona he still feels a great sense of pride and loss for.

"He was at the peak of his career," he said. "He was becoming the premier reliever in the National League."

His voice appearing to break slightly, Umbricht added a footnote about his brother, whom he still recalls with great love: "He was liked by everybody, he did not dislike anybody. And, he finally made it to the major leagues—that was the important thing."

As an added footnote, the Astrodome, like Umbricht's retired uniform number, also became controversial. The Astros vacated the domed stadium in 2000 and now play at Minute Maid Park, which opened as Enron Field. In 2013 voters turned down a bond issue that would have authorized $217 million to convert the aging domed stadium into an event and convention center, meaning the stadium will likely be demolished. If that occurs, Umbricht's ashes may someday rest beneath a parking garage.

12

Three for Three

*The crowd and its team had finally understood that in
games, as in many things, the ending, the final score, is only
part of what matters. The process, the pleasure, the grain
of the game count, too.*
—*Thomas Boswell, columnist,* Washington Post

Ralph Kiner: Powell on the mound, getting set to
work the eighth inning. First man up will be John Paciorek, playing in right field. John has a perfect game
going: He looks at the first pitch, it's strike one.

Horace Greeley, the great nineteenth-century newspaper editor,
once remarked, "Journalism will kill you, but it will keep you alive
while you're at it." The same can be said for baseball. Consider the
extensive travel that modern-day baseball requires and the necessity
of flying between cities, often once or twice a week. The pressure,
too, can be daunting as players walk a fine line between success and
failure each day that they're in the big leagues, knowing that an injury or a prolonged slump can send them back home in search of a

new career. During his first day on the job Paciorek was experiencing that pressure to excel, and through seven and a half innings he had performed superbly. In the late innings, with a Colt victory a fait accompli, the pressure was diminishing. For Paciorek the day had evolved into one of exhilaration, muted only by the knowledge that his back was still an issue and probably would be long into the off season. What journalist Greeley failed to mention were the intangibles that keep people such as Paciorek striving in a business, a craft, that "will kill you" *and* "keep you alive" at the same time. In baseball the thrill of winning, the camaraderie that players enjoy while on the field, and the joy of playing alongside other great players are a few of those intangibles. How long Paciorek's success as a major leaguer would last was anybody's guess, but the way things were going it would last forever. Or, perhaps, just a day—a very unforgettable day.

With a rare called strike on a Powell slider, Paciorek's final at-bat in a career that he would remember as both glorious and inglorious was under way. He was leading off with his team ahead 13–4, and finally, almost in passing, Kiner had reported to his listeners just what they were tuned in to: a perfect game. The term is rarely used in the context of great hitting, except when a player hits for the cycle—a home run, triple, double, and single in the same game. The immutable Paciorek was breaking the mold. So far he *was* perfect: 2 for 2, three RBI, four runs scored, two putouts in right field, and two clean plays on base hits to the outfield. His batting average at that point? Still 1.000. On-base percentage? 1.000. Slugging percentage? Likewise. Fielding average? Ditto. Perfection. His motivation to excel at the big-league level was having the desired impact.

"There were three times when I really felt like a big leaguer: at Wrigley Field, when I took batting practice for Paul Richards; in minor-league training ball at Moultrie, Georgia; and in that one major-league game. If there was any conscious motivation to do something in that game it was the instant I knew I was playing. I don't know whether I'd have felt the same way if Sandy Koufax or Nolan Ryan had been pitching."

Paciorek had no way of knowing, but whether he succeeded in this, his final at-bat, would determine whether he would be remembered as the greatest one-game wonder that professional baseball had ever known, or whether he would soon be forgotten, tossed into a memory bin for all time along with lesser one-game perfect hitters, men like Mike Hopkins (2 for 2), Hal Deviney (2 for 2), and Harry "Doc" Tonkin (2 for 2). If he made out in the eighth Aubrey Epps would remain the disputed leader of the One-Game Career Club.

> **Kiner:** Paciorek has walked twice and singled twice
> in his debut in the major leagues. He has scored three
> runs [Kiner was in error—Paciorek had actually scored
> four runs] in the ball game. And the next pitch is low
> for ball one—one ball, one strike.

As the next pitch sailed in, a ball to even the count, Kiner wasn't ready to publicly rave about Paciorek's sterling debut, although he said fifty years later that at the time he probably was thinking, *What a way to start!* His calm at Paciorek's great debut might be explained simply: In the early 1960s the banter that play-by-play announcers delivered to listeners was less verbose than it is today, as broadcasters spent most of their time calling the actual play on the field rather than filling airtime with statistics. So, too, Kiner may not have fully appreciated that he and his broadcast cohorts were watching history being made in the midst of a game that featured two terribly bad teams. A relatively inexperienced announcer, he probably assumed Paciorek would return the following season, and many seasons after that, and that what he was witnessing was simply one of numerous great games that the young man would enjoy over the course of his career. Still, the boy from Detroit probably deserved more attention than he was getting. For instance, how did he get to the big leagues so quickly? Whose démarche was it to start him that day—was it manager Craft's decision, or owner Hofheinz's, or did the move result from the insistence of an executive, such as GM Richards or assistant GM Robinson? Or was it idiopathic, for no apparent reason, which seems unlikely? What about his injured back—was there any fear of him permanently damaging it? Was Craft concerned that throwing Paciorek into the starting lineup with such dispatch might overwhelm his green rookie?

Probably not. Craft—Aspromonte called him "my stepfather, he really took care of me"—had worked with young players before, managing two of the best in baseball history: Mickey Mantle, a Hall of Fame center fielder for the Yankees, and onetime single-season home run record holder Maris, both early on in their careers. In the early 1960s Mantle and Maris had terrorized opponents as the most feared one–two punch in baseball, and in some ways Paciorek had modeled himself after The Mick, although not in a way that benefited him physically.

"The thing that always impressed me about Mantle was his neck," he once said. "I used to do some crazy exercises to build up my neck. At one point I had a 19.5-inch neck, but I would do so many stupid exercises that I'd actually hurt myself. I used to do headstands—sometimes I'd slip and be incapacitated for a couple of weeks because I couldn't move my neck."[59]

Coincidentally, Tom Paciorek described his brother's power as "maybe just a dash below a Mickey Mantle. It was nothing for John to hit a five-hundred-foot ball—he was freakish from a power stand-point. He would've had a very productive career, and had he reached the potential that everybody thought he had, boy, it could've been a fifteen-, sixteen-, or seventeen-year career."

Although Mantle and Maris had slugged fifty-four and sixty-one homers, respectively, in 1961, the year that Maris broke Babe Ruth's single-season home run mark, their numbers would begin to decline starting in 1962, when Maris would hit thirty-three home runs and Mantle thirty. Craft's stock also was declining, and the 1964 season would be his final one as a major-league manager.

Born in Ellisville, Mississippi, Craft attended Mississippi State College in Clinton before making his major-league debut with the Cincinnati Reds late in the 1937 season. Nicknamed "Wildfire," he was just twenty-two but played well given the limited action he saw during his rookie season: playing in ten games he hit .310 with two doubles, a triple, and four RBI. The following season he was the Reds' regular center fielder, hitting a solid .270 with fifteen home runs and eighty-three RBI. After that his batting average, home runs, and RBI totals drifted downward until in 1942 he hit just .177 and drove in only six runners. He spent the 1943 and 1944 seasons in the military and never made it back to the major leagues as a player.

While he did return as a manager, that did not occur until after he had paid his dues as a skipper in the minor leagues. Mantle began his career under Craft's tutelage, playing for him in 1949 while with Independence, Kansas, of the Kansas–Oklahoma–Missouri League and the following season with Joplin, Missouri, of the

Western Association. Maris played for Craft later on, when he managed the Kansas City Athletics in 1958 and 1959. Maris said the young skipper helped him become a better hitter[60]—a high compliment coming from a man whose name is synonymous with home runs.

Craft also managed the Cubs before Houston hired him as the team's first manager in 1962. He continued managing the Colts through the 1963 season and most of 1964. However, the club fired him with thirteen games left on the schedule.

Craft's swift elevation of Paciorek had to be one of the most propitious moves in baseball history, even though it failed to have any lasting effect—except for the single-game career mark. By bringing up a teen with only minimal minor-league experience, thrusting him into the starting lineup of a major-league club, and letting him sink or swim, Craft proved it is sometimes easier to do the butterfly than summon a lifeguard. Additionally, just two days earlier, on September 27, 1963, Craft had famously started nine rookies, the majority of whom were not in the lineup with Paciorek on the final day of the season just two days later; among the starters in Craft's much-publicized rookie lineup were Brock Davis, Aaron Pointer, Sonny Jackson, Jay Dahl, and Jerry Grote, along with Wynn, Staub, Morgan, and Vaughan. Any second thoughts or even guilt Craft may have had about his youth movement were probably expended long before Paciorek ever played an inning. If not, they were quickly expiated when the young right fielder began hitting the baseball with the skill of a proven veteran.

As Paciorek waited for the next pitch his performance was beginning to resonate with Kiner, who moments earlier had noted, "John has a perfect game going"—neither he nor Nelson had offered much more than that during Paciorek's previous four at-bats, although Nelson had proffered a short biography when he introduced him prior to his first at-bat in the second inning: "John Paciorek is coming up for his first time in the major leagues. Paciorek is eighteen years of age, six foot two, a two-hundred-pounder from Detroit, Michigan. He hit .219 in seventy-eight games at Modesto this season with nine homers and forty-nine runs batted in." End of story, at least for the moment.

> **Kiner:** Pitch back to him, a swing and a miss—strike two. One ball, two strikes.

Behind on the count, tired, weary, sweaty, dirty, and pumped up all at the same time, Paciorek was enjoying his final at bat. Each time up to the plate had been a high note for the strapping outfielder, but he wanted to end things with an exclamation point: his third hit. He watched the pitcher Powell, who at five ten and 175 pounds appeared anything but physically intimidating. Still, with thirty-nine strikeouts in forty-nine innings Powell could "bring the ball," as the players say. The question in Paciorek's mind was, what would he bring? Ahead on the batter, the odds were that Powell would come back with a curveball, figuring the teen hadn't seen many big-league "roundhouses" and that the state of weariness—or perhaps overconfidence—he presumed the young man was experiencing might tempt him into swinging at a pitch that he couldn't drive. The odds proved correct.

> **Kiner:** Should correct ourselves, Paciorek has scored four runs, he's been on base four times and scored every time. The pitch back to the plate is low, a curveball, two

balls and two strikes.

With the count even the historical significance of what the broadcast team was watching had become clear: raw perfection in the rookie right fielder.

> **Kiner:** Can't have a better debut in baseball than to be up four times, score four runs, and come off perfect at 2 for 2 with two walks. Next pitch, a hard ground ball off the glove of [third baseman] Ted Schreiber, he can't find the ball. Paciorek rounds at first base and holds there, and this one could go as a base hit.

Kiner was short on a couple of counts. He had omitted Paciorek's three RBI, which fueled the Colts' big lead, and he would soon learn it *is* possible to have a better debut than 2 for 2. Paciorek proved that by bouncing a ground ball off the glove of Schreiber. That left the rookie's fate up to the official scorer: would he call it a hit, sending Paciorek dancing into the record books, or would he rule it an error on the twenty-five-year-old rookie infielder, who also was playing in his final major-league game? Schreiber, a native of Brooklyn, New York, would end his career with a .160 batting average in thirty-nine games and fewer RBI—two—and runs scored—1—than Paciorek achieved in his only major-league game.

"It's scored as a hit!" Kiner said. "So John Paciorek has a perfect day going—he's reached first base in his first five appearances in the major leagues. Three times on base hits, two times on walks."

In Paciorek's mind there never was any doubt that the scorer would rule it a hit, especially with his speed.

"I thought it was a clean base hit," he said. "He dove for it and knocked it down. There's no way that would have been an error."

With the scorer's ruling, Paciorek was nearly ready to tie a bow on his parboiled major-league career. The rookie Adlesh, who was 0 for 7 on the season, would hit for the catcher Bateman, grounding the ball to pitcher Powell, who would turn a pitcher-to-second-base-to-first-base double play—sending Paciorek back to the dugout for the last time in his career.

"I didn't know he got three hits until after the game," said Rusty Staub, who went 1 for 4 with one RBI that day. "I was really happy for him, he looked good.

"When you think back on the potential that was there . . ."

Paciorek believes that at that point, although the game was not over, he probably was aware of his hit total for the afternoon. "It's hard to believe I wasn't aware of it," he said.

Two batters later pitcher Jim Dickson, hitting for himself with a big lead, would foul out to Schreiber at third and the Colts were done, at least offensively: no runs, one hit, no errors, none left on base. New York had one more at-bat left, but there was little chance the lowly Metropolitans would overcome a nine-run lead to win the final game of the season—even against the also-lowly Colts.

As he ran to his position in the outfield—he always sprinted on and off the field—Paciorek knew he would not bat again that day, or that season. He had no way of knowing, however, that he would never again swing at a major-league pitch. He would never catch another ball, or have an opportunity to prevent a runner from scoring with a dazzling throw. Other than the few practice tosses he would receive from center fielder Murrell as the players warmed up for the final half inning of play, he would not touch a baseball again in the major leagues. The Mets would go down quietly in the top half of the ninth with Kranepool hitting into a double play after rookie pinch hitter Dick Smith had batted for the pitcher Powell with one out and singled. The game was over, the Colts had won, and Paciorek was gone from the game that he assumed would pay the bills for many years to come.

"My back hurt throughout the game, but I managed to put it out of my mind for nine innings," said Paciorek. "I really enjoyed the experience, and as the game went on I really felt pretty good. I was anxious for more of the same the following season.

"The last one was my best hit. The first two were Texas Leaguers."

Although the accolades would pour in, as they would for any rookie who enjoyed such a sensational debut, Paciorek would quietly fade into the shadows after the season ended. Still, no one could take away from the likable Hamtramckian what he had accomplished.

"It certainly is [an unusual accomplishment]," Kiner said of Paciorek's 3 for 3 game fifty years later. "It's a strange thing, as a matter of fact—three hits and three runs batted in and to not play again . . ." He added, "It's never happened before or since."

Little-known Joe Gaines would occupy right field for much of the 1964 season, finishing with a respectable .254 batting average with seven home runs and thirty-four RBI. Those numbers would be good enough to earn him another look in 1965, when his average would fall to .227. In 1966 he would hit .077 and that would be it for the twenty-nine-year-old outfielder. By then, Paciorek and his one-game hit-and-RBI fest would be little more than a memory to most of the fans in attendance that day. The briefly spectacular one-game career of John Paciorek, the muscular right fielder with loads of talent, a can't-miss career, and a bum back, was over.

"It's impressive," said two-gamer Workman, the former Yankee whose one and only hit came in his fourth of five major-league at bats. "Either impressive or lucky."

Tom Paciorek put his brother's feat in perspective. "I'm sure he'd trade it for a ten-year career hitting .250. For being the answer to a trivia question I think it's a real neat thing. It's cool, it really is. Millions of people wish they'd had the opportunity to play in one game. John had the ability to play thousands of major-league games, but it just wasn't going to happen."

In 140 years some twenty thousand men have played baseball at the major-league level; of those, fewer than one thousand played in only one game.[61] Through 2010 only eighty-seven players had batted 1.000: seventy-seven were 1 for 1, nine were 2 for 2, and only one player collected three hits in three at-bats: Paciorek. Kiner, who knew both Babe Ruth and Ty Cobb, said: "There's a guy who of all the players who have played in the major leagues, he did something that not even Babe Ruth, Ty Cobb, or any other ballplayer has done. That's one of those odd records."

Ex-Yankee Workman, a longtime Los Angeles attorney, described it more succinctly: Paciorek, he said, was "perfect."

As recently as 2012 Paciorek could still recall the excitement of, as Kiner put it, that "odd" record, playing before a home crowd on that warm summer day when John F. Kennedy was president but the country was only eight weeks away from changing forever.

"The thing I remember most is how exciting it was that the crowd was giving me special applause as I came to bat for my final turn," said Paciorek, who received a standing ovation prior to his fifth at-bat. "It seemed like a million people, but in reality it was only a few thousand. It was the biggest crowd I had ever played for."[62] He added: "I didn't dominate the pitchers, I didn't hit line shots off the wall or anything like that."

> **Kiner**: That's the end of the season. Final score of
> the ballgame: the Colts 13, the Mets 4. So long for the
> year.

For the fans, for all who were listening in New York, Houston, and the many communities on the periphery of those broadcast markets, it was so long for the season. For John Paciorek, the indisputable star of the game, it was so long forever.

13

Yesterdays

Let's play two.
—Ernie Banks, infielder

John Paciorek would not "play two"—only one. Yesterday began the moment the right fielder Kranepool grounded into a game-ending double play. With his debut game now in the books, Paciorek trotted off the field to the delight of fans and teammates and disappeared into the dugout. If he hadn't been keeping personal statistics in his head—and many ballplayers do not—it would not take long for him to learn the magnificence of the numbers he had transacted that day. They were perfect: three hits, three RBI, four runs scored, a perfect batting average, a perfect fielding average, and a perfect on-base percentage. He had done all that Craft could have hoped for when the manager, at some risk, penciled his name into the starting lineup that afternoon. Thanks largely to his own exploits Paciorek's team had won the ballgame by a resounding margin, 13–4. In the spirit of Ernie Banks, Paciorek probably would've liked to play another game. That wouldn't happen.

With the sun low over downtown Houston and the rooftops beginning to cool, it was time for America's newest major-league base-ball star to return to the Surrey House restaurant, eat some dinner, retire to his room, relax in front of the television, look ahead to re-pairing his injured back, and anticipate the 1964 season and all the possibilities it held in store for him. In all likelihood, and by his own declaration many years later, Paciorek was the man to beat if anyone else in the Houston organization had designs on playing right field for the Colts the following season—there certainly would be others, including Gaines. Nevertheless, he had to feel good about his stand-ing on what then was a very young and promising club, one that had a chance of winning the National League pennant or even the World Series as its young players continued to mature during the ensuing seasons.

"I was projected to be the center fielder for [Houston] for the next generation," he told writer Thomas Wayne in a 2009 interview. "The organization gave me every opportunity to be their next su-perstar."[63]

Despite his impressive debut and the praise he had collected, es-pecially from the news media, Paciorek was worried. The bad back remained a serious, even career-threatening, issue, and he knew it.

"I recall thinking, *How am I going to do this?* How could I con-tinue to play with the constant fear that was there all the time?" Meanwhile, "I was still doing handstands, still working on my neck."

The answer to his question was . . . he *couldn't* continue to do it. For Paciorek, a career in the major leagues, let alone superstardom, was not in the cards—just as continuing their own careers wasn't in the cards for three other popular ballplayers: Musial, Hubbs, and teammate Umbricht. On September 29, 1963, unique yesterdays were established for those three as well. In St. Louis, Dal Maxvill

Itching to hit again while recuperating
following back operation, 1964

doubled in Ernie Broglio in the bottom of the fourteenth inning to nail down the Cardinals' 3–2 win over Cincinnati. With that victory, Stan Musial had played in his final game, retiring from baseball to enjoy life as a successful restaurateur and high-profile baseball ambassador.

In Milwaukee, Santo also hit into a game-ending double play, securing the Braves' 2–0 win over the Cubs. Although Hubbs had an off day at the plate, failing to get a base hit, he, like Paciorek, had the highest of hopes for what he might accomplish during the following season. Those hopes would soon turn to dust in the swollen debris of his fractured airplane.

Like Paciorek, teammate Umbricht also must have been satisfied with his play against the Mets that afternoon, although for him there were more pressing battles to wage than taking a vacation or planning a workout regimen in preparation for the 1964 baseball season. Although Umbricht had been the Colts' winning pitcher, his cancer remained a formidable opponent as he walked to the Houston locker room. As his teammates looked ahead to a period of rest and relaxation, Umbricht's full-time "job" was to beat the disease that threatened to curtail his career and end his life, and ultimately he would fail. He, too, had played in his last major-league game, the victim of a relentless disease that swallowed him up in the prime of life. Paciorek, Musial, Hubbs, and Umbricht: four very different endings to four very different careers—all on the final day of the 1963 season.

In 2014, only one of the four survives: Paciorek.

"It was great," Paciorek reminisced about the game with Sarah Nelson, a writer for Christian Science JSH Online. "I'd driven myself hard to reach [my] goal, devoting every ounce of my energy to get into the big leagues."[64] He added, "I enjoyed immensely the opportunity to play. You can't appreciate something like that until it's been put into posterity for 50 or 60 years."

For other players in the Mets–Colts game there also was some doubt, and over time that date—September 29, 1963—would resonate as *their* final day in the major leagues. Those who had suited up for the last time included Paciorek's teammate Vaughan and Mets players Schreiber, Joe Hicks, Chico Fernandez, and Powell. For them, as for Paciorek, baseball became a thing of the past—their yesterday.

That night and the following day Paciorek's name seemed to be everywhere: on the television news, in newspaper articles, and, presumably, on the minds of the Houston players and front office personnel, some of whom prematurely pronounced him the team's star of the future.

"I turned on the television set in the team hotel room and a sports announcer was predicting I had a long career ahead of me," Paciorek said, noting that the *Houston Post* went so far as to infer there was no way he could fail to make it in the major leagues.

Based upon his one-day performance, at some level Paciorek felt the same sense of optimism, although it proved to be misplaced. There was no arrogance—he simply understood his own strength and ability, as did others along the continuum he chased.

"Whenever we talk about top prospects who had the tools and the strengths but didn't enjoy the success we had envisioned, John's name is always mentioned," said Tal Smith, who served as director of player personnel for the Colts when Paciorek played and was with the team for more than three decades.[65]

In a story that appeared in many newspapers the following day, the Associated Press wrote, "Eighteen-year-old John Paciorek was the game's star in his first big league appearance. He had a perfect afternoon."[66] The *New York Times* proclaimed that Paciorek "found nothing difficult about the majors—or at least about the Mets,"[67] continuing, "[He] doesn't yet know what it's like to make an out in the big leagues." In its own interpretation of the game the now-defunct *Houston Post*, which conferred upon Paciorek, with tongue in check, the unofficial major-league batting title, suggested, "The rest of [Paciorek's] career may be an anticlimax." Of all the newspapers that announced Paciorek's success during the days that followed the close of the 1963 baseball season, the *Post* put it the most succinctly: The remainder of Paciorek's career *was* an anticlimax, although it was resurrected decades later and continues to sizzle in trivia circles and online.

"It's incredible, " Aspromonte said. "To accomplish that in one game, and to do that in his *only* game, carries a lot of feelings. To think that he was able to do that, and it was his last game, and he had to walk away from it . . ." His voice trailed off.

After the season ended, Paciorek's back continued to cause him severe discomfort, resonating "like a knife stabbing me." However, he hid the extent of his problem from the Colts. He exercised faithfully and with great energy in an effort to ameliorate a condition he later described as "irreparable,"[68] expecting it to magically improve over a period of weeks or months. The magic never came. Still, Paciorek's confidence remained high. He had lived with the injury since the middle of his season with Modesto, and as a young man who was otherwise fit he continued to believe the pain would ebb over time. It didn't.

"I knew I belonged in the big leagues, so I kept hoping for the best," he said. "But I was always in great pain, especially when I went

Sketch of Paciorek, 2014
(Courtesy of Kailie Barnes)

down to field balls."[69]

As expected, the Colts welcomed Paciorek to spring training with open arms prior to the 1964 season, giving him every opportunity to make the big club as its starting right fielder. However, as spring training progressed and the regular season approached the pain remained, greatly limiting his mobility both in the outfield and at the plate. As a result his overall play deteriorated. The Colts, still unaware of the severity of his condition and the chronic pain it was causing, sent him down to the team's Class A Durham Bulls and later to the Statesville Colts, also in Class A, for some seasoning. It was at Durham where Paciorek last played with Raymond Ferrand, whose baseball career ended when a golf ball struck him in the face, blinding one eye.

"He was a good-sized kid and he kept in real good shape," Ferrand said. "We played together in Durham, and one day a storm came through and knocked a section of the left field fence down. He hit two home runs in the same spot, through the fence and not over it—the umpires missed both calls."

The demotions to Durham and then Statesville failed to have the intended result—Paciorek played in only forty-nine games with the two teams, hitting .155 at Durham with four home runs and twelve RBI and .063 for Statesville with just one RBI. Instead of improving, things were getting worse, and the pain was now becoming unbearable. Finally, as a last resort, Paciorek revealed his injury to the team and in mid-season underwent spinal fusion surgery at Houston Methodist Hospital, which left him bedridden for nearly a month and required he wear a metal back brace for the next year—a period during which his weight dropped from 210 pounds to 160; later, an impromptu visit to the boisterous Houston locker room hushed the noisy players as they observed the slugger's deteriorated physique upon entering.

Although the Colts graciously placed him on the major-league roster so that he could collect $7,500 in salary, for John Paciorek

Posing with back brace following surgery, 1964

the 1964 season was over. The only hope for salvaging his once-promising professional baseball career was a methodical recovery.

Paciorek missed the entire 1965 season as well—his only inactive year in professional baseball. He attempted a comeback in 1966 with the Class A Batavia Trojans and the Salisbury Astros, hitting .158 and .247—not the kind of numbers that attract serious interest from major-league ball clubs. He did, however, hit six home runs and drive in forty-one runs; Houston, impressed by those numbers, decided to stick with him awhile longer.

Unfortunately, the back pain persisted, exacerbated by the recurrence of an old shoulder injury and a series of hamstring muscle problems. At the same time, the realization that his career in baseball might be over began to creep into his thoughts. Not only was Paciorek damaged physically, but the injuries were now affecting his psyche, not good in a sport where success is determined as much by the mind—confidence—as it is by the body and its ability to perform. Still, he was just twenty-one years old, an age when many players have yet to receive any serious attention from the major-league teams that own them and oversee their progress and their futures. By most standards Paciorek was still ahead of the game. He had tasted success, knew what was required, and believed that his best years lay ahead of him. If only he could shake the physical demons that were beating up on him every time he came to the plate, scurried toward a batted ball, or attempted to throw a runner out.

The back injury became so painful that at one point Paciorek was unable to hit curveballs, and to compensate he became a switch hitter. The experiment failed miserably. His numbers in 1967 for the Class A Asheville Tourists and the Cocoa Astros were even worse than they were in 1966: In thirty-two games he hit just .128 with one home run and two RBI for Asheville and 0.50 without any home runs or RBI for Cocoa. Just four years after breaking in as a can't-miss right fielder for a major-league organization, Paciorek was released by Houston. His career appeared to be over—but not quite.

"As long as I had hope I was going to continue," he said.[70]

Out of baseball and with time on his hands, Paciorek began spending afternoons watching his brother Tom play for the University of Houston, where the younger Paciorek had become a star football and baseball player. One day while he was watching Tom perform, a Cleveland Indians scout recognized John, introduced himself and eventually took a chance and signed him to a minor-league contract. It was 1968 and the twenty-three-year-old outfielder had one more opportunity to fulfill his dream of fighting his way back up to the major leagues.

Fight he did, working harder than he ever had. It paid off. In 1968 Paciorek had his best season ever with the Class A Reno Silver Sox, hitting .275 and slugging seventeen home runs while driving in sixty-five runs. With those numbers on his résumé he earned his first assignment in AA ball, with the Rock Hill Indians, that same year. However, injuries reared up again: He dislocated two fingers on a play in the outfield, then tore his Achilles tendon. After just twenty-three games the Indians also released him. His overall minor-league record up until that point? A .209 batting average in 360 games, with forty-four home runs and 191 RBI. At the age of twenty-three it was time to hang up his cleats.

"When I realized that no matter how much stretching and preparation I would do before games and practices I would still pull or tear muscles, I gave up all hope of reaching my destiny," he said. "I was relieved when the Cleveland Indians finally released me during my last desperate [opportunity]."[71]

In five short years Paciorek's fortunes had shifted dramatically. He had gone from starting right fielder for a major-league team, performing so solidly that management invited him to return for spring training the following season, to being cut summarily by two major-league franchises. His back hurt, he was disappointed, and it wasn't yet clear how he would earn a living. Still, as he began to feel better his thoughts once again turned to baseball.

"It seemed like I was through, but I couldn't be sure," he said. "I had remained in good physical shape and my back was no longer hurting. I didn't want to leave baseball, but from a practical standpoint I knew I needed a backup plan."

Despite his willingness to catch on with whoever would take him, after years of pushing through pain and physical uncertainty Paciorek was resigned: for him, baseball was over. A seesaw career that had started in the low minor leagues, rocketed him to the major leagues, dropped him just as fast back down into single-A ball, then teased him briefly by boosting him up a notch to his only double-A assignment, had ended. Out of options, out of major-league teams interested in the services of a man with a 1.000 lifetime batting average, Paciorek would go no further in the game he loved but that somehow had become bittersweet. The man from Detroit and Hamtramck, whose swing was magical for the briefest period, was through with the sport, ready to move on with his life. His athletic denouement had played out and it was time for him to find another line of work, one that didn't involve hitting a stitched orb thrown at light speed. Metaphorically, Paciorek took his ball and went home.

Epilogue

John Paciorek

As he sat out the 1965 season with the expectation of fully re-covering from back surgery and continuing with his seesaw baseball career, perhaps even at the major-league level, Paciorek decided to make the most of a negative situation by enrolling in classes at the University of Houston, where he—like his brother Tom—eventually would earn a degree. There had been scholarship opportunities as his high school career came to a close, but the Houston organization convinced him that with his skills he would never need to rely on the benefits tendered by a college education. Even so, the team had set up a scholarship for him—just in case. "In retrospect, that was the most important thing the Colts offered me," he said. It paid big dividends. While temporarily out of baseball he completed two years of college at the university where he'd once wanted to play ball and laid the groundwork for a different career, one that has lasted nearly four decades.

That would not be his only foray onto the sprawling, athletically charged campus. Fast-forward to 1967 on the same university grounds, where a Cleveland Indians scout would "discover" Paciorek just when it appeared his career was over. With the tumultuous '60s in full swing and the country inching toward a second Kennedy as-sassination, that of Senator Robert F. Kennedy in 1968, Paciorek was again taking classes. In his spare time he was watching his little

Appearing fit, at least outwardly, following back surgery, 1964

brother Tom play solid ball for the Cougar baseball team. The following year, in the 1968 amateur draft, Tom would be chosen in
the fifth round by the Los Angeles Dodgers, and his signing would
pave the way for him to play in 1,392 games—1,391 more than
John had played in during his short-lived career.

For whatever reason, Paciorek felt comfortable on the UH campus, which was situated just seven miles from Colt Stadium, and
each time he returned there the school yielded good results for him.
One of those results was a lifelong spiritual interest, which began in
the fall of 1967 when the "can't-miss kid," who at that time was

again out of baseball, stopped by the campus religious center. It was close to Thanksgiving and the only door that was open led into a small, quiet, dimly lit Christian Science reading room. Paciorek, still searching for the secret to stability and hope and willing to look beyond Catholicism to find those intangibles, walked inside. Once there he scanned the various shelves of material. He began to read.

"The things I read touched something inside of me—it seemed like I had found something I had been searching for over many years," Paciorek said. "At last everything made sense, and the impression was indelible."

The words almost jumped off the pages, making such a weighty impression on the lifelong Catholic that Paciorek eventually joined the church. He finished his studies at the University of Houston in the early 1970s, earning a degree in physical education, and became a physical education instructor at the Jewish Community Center in Houston, where Rusty Staub later trained and became better acquainted with his former roommate. After several years there his first wife, Linda, who would later die of breast cancer, told him she had heard about a teaching opportunity at a parochial school just outside Los Angeles. Paciorek applied for the job, was hired by administrators, and in 1976 began work at the Clairbourn School, where he remains an active and popular member of the school faculty. Now remarried and a grandfather many times over, Paciorek, the father of eight children—five from his first marriage, one from his second, and two stepchildren, also from his second—lives in a comfortable home in San Gabriel, where his second wife, Karen, a longtime administrator at Clairbourn, was reared. Life is good for major-league baseball's greatest 1.000 hitter.

Paciorek's career and the disillusionment that encumbered him were little known around the picturesque Clairbourn campus for many years. Even the children on the baseball, basketball, and track teams he has coached knew little or nothing about the triumph of his only major-league game—it seldom came up in classroom conversation or on the playground and ball field, although more recently it has. "They say I'm the greatest guy who ever played," he said.[72]

Eventually, his coveted privacy took a hit. A freelance journalist digging through piles of baseball statistics confirmed that Paciorek's big day at Colt Stadium represented the finest single-game career in major-league baseball history. The reporter wanted to know what happened and why it all ended so abruptly, and he wanted to tell Paciorek's story on the pages of the *Los Angeles Times*. Although slightly reluctant, Paciorek consented and publicly related his unique baseball narrative to this writer for perhaps the first time.

The 1,089-word article was published twenty-eight years after Paciorek played for the Colts, and in the years after it first appeared there were many such encounters with inquisitive writers. Each story elicited the same basic information: that Paciorek had indeed experienced the greatest one-day career in major-league baseball history, that a back injury had derailed his otherwise promising future in the big leagues, and that he did have regrets about "retiring" while the mud on his cleats was still damp.

"I certainly have regrets about the way things turned out . . . the hope of playing in the major leagues for a long time was something I had cherished. Had I not been injured and in pain I have no doubt I would have been a success at the major-league level—nothing short of that would have been acceptable to me. After fifty years I still have people ask me about my perfect game."

The game itself aside, a curious point of interest bisects his baseball life after September 29, 1963: the assassination of President Kennedy fifty-four days later, on November 22 of that same year. Until that juncture he was on an uphill trajectory that culminated on the field at Colt Stadium. Then the 1963 season ended, Kennedy was tragically murdered just 225 miles from the ballpark, and the following season Paciorek's career began to unravel like the yarn inside a beaten-up hardball. The demarcation is a curious one: The death of Kennedy and the demise of Paciorek's baseball career starkly coincide.

While Paciorek's career was a short one, there was some carryover. Son Pete played nine seasons of minor-league ball beginning in 1995, clawing his way up to double A on three different occasions. Another son, Mack, competed in the minor leagues from 2000 to 2004. Certainly their father had some advice to offer his boys along the way—about how to succeed in the sport and how to know when it's time to give up the coveted dream. After all, every ballplayer has his own recipe for life and success, even for failure. Paciorek's is both philosophical and retrospective.

"If my baseball career had panned out I might not have married or had children," he said. "With a healthy, pain-free back I might have ended up in Vietnam and perhaps even gotten killed. Success in baseball might have brought me considerable fortune, and I might not have handled my money wisely. The way things turned out I ended up taking a different route, and in that I found a spiritual transformation."

Not that his baseball "career" doesn't continue to hold relevance beyond the one box score that lists his name. As a college student Paciorek's niece completed an exam, and afterward the instructor asked the class of perhaps a hundred students a question for extra credit: what ballplayer went 3 for 3 in his only major-league game? One hand went up, and when the surprised professor asked her how she knew the answer she responded, "He's my uncle." Indeed, for more than fifty years Paciorek has surprised people everywhere with his single-game achievement. It's a legacy like no other, and Paciorek is widely considered the crown jewel of one-game wonders.

"I've been asked about it hundreds of times," brother Tom Paciorek said.

Perhaps author Richard Tellis said it best in *Once Around the Bases*: "John Paciorek's performance in his one game in the major leagues almost makes you shake your head in disbelief."[73] General manager Richards was probably one of few who were not shaking their heads in disbelief. When Paciorek signed with Houston, Richards predicted that his young signatory "could become one of the really great power hitters and all-around players in baseball."[74]

In an interview with this writer, actor Jack Larson, who was hopelessly typecast as overeager reporter Jimmy Olsen on the *Adventures of Superman* television series, discussed the obituary that he envisions will someday follow his own death. Larson, who was mindful of the many other achievements he had made during long and successful careers as both an actor and writer and eventually came to appreciate the unique role that has long been associated with him, said, "I know that . . . when they write my obituary it will say, 'Jack Larson, best remembered on the popular *Adventures of Superman* series.' I'm pleased with it, I'm proud of it, and I would certainly do it again. It's nice not to be forgotten."

Certainly Paciorek, like Larson, is satisfied with the matchless accomplishment that defines him as a baseball player. He is pleased and proud and would gladly do it all over again despite the many disappointments he encountered along the way. In a very real sense Paciorek earned the record with every ounce of physicality he had, and the mark is something he will always treasure.

"Oh, yeah!" he said when asked whether he is glad he played that day despite the debilitating outcome. "Eventually, the same thing would have happened anyway."

Perhaps Wynn, who retired in 1977 with 291 career home runs, summed up Paciorek's dazzling debut—indeed, his *career*—the best: "For a man who did not play that long, that's one heckuva feat. Anybody would like *that* [kind of debut], *I'd* even take *that*. That's batting 1.000!"

Despite having the cherished number "1.000" firmly in the pocket of his baseball flannels, representing the ultimate in perfection, Paciorek remains a former big-league ballplayer with a major-league asterisk beside his name—and a batting average second to none: not to Cobb, or Hornsby, or Williams, or Speaker, or Shoeless Joe Jackson, each of them great hitters. All in all, for a guy with only three major-league at-bats, it's nice not to be forgotten.

"It's kind of a dubious honor," Paciorek said. "But I guess I'm immortalized. I did something no one else has ever done."

Ethan Chapman, who in 2014 began his first season of double-A ball as an outfielder with the Kansas City Royals organization, hopes to play in the big leagues himself someday. Like Paciorek once did, Chapman is aiming for a long and successful career, hoping the journey that takes him there, however circuitous, will prove fruitful sooner rather than later. He understands the challenge that lies ahead and has great respect for Paciorek, who traveled the same difficult path half a century ago, one that for him paid off—if only for a nano-season. Chapman's words spoke for minor leaguers everywhere.

"John Paciorek accomplished something that every kid who grows up playing baseball dreams about: playing in the major leagues," he said. "Even though it was only for one game, it's an amazing accomplishment."

Like Chapman, Ryan Ledbetter, a single-A pitcher with the Texas Rangers organization, also dreams of playing in the major leagues. He considers those dreams a forerunner to eventually pitching on a big-league team and has great respect for Paciorek's fast ascent. "We don't just dream of making it to the major leagues, we put in years of hard work to get there," he said. "John has something to be extremely proud of. What he accomplished is truly remarkable."

Aubrey Epps

The likelihood that Epps would not return to the major leagues after his debut game in 1935 effectively became reality seven years later when he was drafted into the military, serving with the Fourth Marine Division and participating in four campaigns in the Pacific Theater of operation during World War II. Epps died in Ackerman, Mississippi, on November 13, 1984, at the age of seventy-two, and is buried at Ackerman Cemetery.

While Epps's name does not appear in most of the contemporary articles that chronicle the best one-game careers in baseball history, he belongs at number two by virtue of his three hits against the Reds—Paciorek is the only other ballplayer to collect as many hits in his only game, while Epps has the distinction of achieving the highest batting average among those who played in only one game but did not bat 1.000. As a footnote, William Edward "Ed" Irvin of the Detroit Tigers falls closely in line behind Epps, going 2 for 3 with two triples on May 18, 1912, during a players strike that resulted when Ty Cobb was suspended for allegedly attacking a fan. A replacement player pulled from the nearby neighborhoods to play for the Tigers that day, Irvin finished his "career" with a .667 batting average and one error. However, his performance was not good enough to earn him a regular spot when the team resumed play and he never again played at the major-league level. When Epps came along and hit .750, Irvin was further embedded in obscurity.

Roy Hofheinz

After the Astrodome opened in 1965, Colt .45s owner Hofheinz continued to develop properties, most notably Astrodomain in Houston, which included a hotel complex. His first wife died the following year and things began to unravel after he suffered a stroke in 1970 at the age of fifty-eight and was confined to a wheelchair. During the next few years Hofheinz's debts accumulated, and in 1976 Astrodomain, a conglomerate that included the Astros, was turned over to creditors after Hofheinz declared bankruptcy. In just over a decade Hofheinz's kingdom had collapsed in a financial pile of rubble. After suffering a heart attack he died at his Houston home on November 22, 1982.

While a quiet maverick in many respects, and a sports, political, judicial, and financial legend in the Lone Star State, Hofheinz's crowning achievement remains creation of the Astrodome, among the first of many domed stadiums that now punctuate the country. His second greatest achievement would have to be his founding ownership of the Houston Colt .45s and later the Astros. Third?

Perhaps it was creating an environment where Paciorek could make his major-league debut on the final day of the 1963 season. Although he may not have had a hand in the decision, the buck certainly stopped with him.

Harry Craft

After Houston fired him toward the end of the 1964 season manager Craft once again reinvented himself, much as he had after his playing days ended in 1942, and started managing in the minor leagues. He returned to baseball in 1967 as a scout for the Yankees, remaining with the team in that capacity until 1972. He then returned to the Astros, again as a scout (1975–77), went back to the Yankees (1978–82), and jumped leagues to the San Francisco Giants (1983–91), retiring in 1991.

In a baseball career that spanned fifty-four years, with a few interruptions along the way, he was a player for six years, all of them with the Cincinnati Reds, a manager in the minors for six years, a manager in the majors for eight seasons, and a scout off and on for another twenty-four years. While his overall managerial record in the major leagues is an inauspicious 353–486, Craft stuck it out for six seasons and holds the distinction of having replaced Hall of Famer Lou Boudreau by signing on to manage the Kansas City Athletics in 1957. He died at the age of eighty in Conroe, Texas, on August 4, 1995, just four years after leaving baseball. Trivia buffs still remember him as having caught a fly ball off the bat of Dodger Leo Durocher to end the ballgame and secure the final out in Vander Meer's second consecutive no-hitter. Vander Meer's record, like Paciorek's, will likely never be broken.

Stan Musial

After retiring from baseball, Musial's jersey number was retired by the St. Louis Cardinals in 1963. While his public presence diminished he remained involved with the Cardinal organization in various capacities during the ensuing years, serving as senior vice president and, briefly, as general manager, leading the organization to a World Series championship in 1967. Two years later, on July 28, 1969, Musial received the ultimate baseball accolade when he was inducted into the Hall of Fame, calling it "the greatest honor of the many that have been bestowed upon me."[75]

Through the years Musial remained involved with numerous investments and his well-known restaurant, Stan Musial and Biggie's, where fans and athletes alike gathered for food and sports conversation. He also served as director for the National Council on Physical Fitness under President Lyndon Johnson. Throughout his retirement Musial was the quintessential ambassador for the game he loved, and a life-sized statue of him posing in his familiar corkscrew stance stands outside Busch Stadium. Until his death at age ninety-two on January 19, 2013, Musial remained—and still remains—a popular St. Louis icon, someone who was just as likely to break into a harmonica riff as flash his warm and engaging smile to a total stranger. Stanislaus Frank "Stan the Man" Musial is resoundingly considered the greatest St. Louis Cardinal of all time.

Tom Paciorek

Nicknamed "Wimpy," Tom Paciorek joined the Dodgers in 1970, the year after his brother John retired from baseball. He remained in the major leagues through the 1987 season, retiring from the Texas Rangers—his sixth team—with a lifetime batting average of .282 and one World Series appearance, in 1974 (he went 1 for 2 in the Series with a double).

After leaving baseball Paciorek worked as a broadcaster, most prominently for the Chicago White Sox from 1988 to 1999. He later broadcast for the Detroit Tigers, Seattle Mariners, Atlanta Braves, and Washington Nationals, the Nationals failing to renew his contract following the 2006 season. His lengthy career and solid, journeyman statistics endear him as a player who made the most of his skills to remain a baseball fixture for nearly two decades. In light of his longevity in the major leagues, Tom Paciorek truly is the anti–John Paciorek.

Jim Paciorek

Born fifteen years after his brother John, Jim Paciorek, who, like John, also was one of the country's top prep prospects, played slightly longer than his sibling: forty-eight games, all of them during brother Tom's final season, 1987. The University of Michigan graduate's numbers were unimpressive and the Milwaukee Brewers released him after a quick look, although he did hit two home runs and drive in ten runners. He credits his brother John for some of his success in reaching the major leagues.

"He used to pitch batting practice to me," he said, then addressed his brother's seemingly untouchable mark: "I'm sure he would much rather have played some more [seasons in the major leagues] than to have the record. That's just the way things worked out."

After his release Jim played in Japan for several years, becoming a top hitter for average although his power was limited. A hip injury shortened his career there, and he attempted a comeback in the United States during the early 1990s. His comeback failed and Jim, like brother John, was soon forgotten.

"Making the [Brewers] was probably the highlight of my career," he said. He then added, with a touch of irony, "I didn't realize it was only going to [last] one year."

Joe Morgan

Joe Morgan was the most successful of the seven rookies who started alongside John Paciorek in the game against the Mets on September 29, 1963. Known affectionately as "Little Joe," Morgan played twenty-two seasons in the major leagues, most of them with Houston and Cincinnati, and retired in 1984 with a lifetime batting average of .271. During his career Morgan recorded more than twenty-five hundred hits while slugging 268 home runs, blasting ninety-six triples, hitting 449 doubles, and knocking in 1,133 runs. Named National League MVP twice, he was elected to the Baseball Hall of Fame in 1990.

After baseball the ten-time all-star became a broadcaster for the Cincinnati Reds in 1985 before embarking on a nine-year stint in the same capacity with the San Francisco Giants the following year. After working for ABC Sports, NBC Sports, ESPN, and Sports USA Radio Network, Morgan opened Joe Morgan Honda in Monroe, Ohio, in 2010. That same year the Reds announced that Morgan would rejoin the club as a special adviser to baseball operations. Thirty-eight years after becoming a Reds player, leading the team to world championships in 1975 and 1976, Morgan had come full circle.

Lindsey Nelson

After leaving the Mets in 1979 Nelson worked three seasons with the San Francisco Giants beginning that same year, and did radio broadcasts for CBS Sports as well. Recognizable for his elegant voice, Nelson also was known for his brilliant attire, in particular his loud sports jackets, and it is believed that he owned hundreds of different coats, many of them plaid.

"He had no tolerance for mistakes," Murphy said in 1995. "He was totally reliable. I don't think he was late once in his whole life."[76]

According to Kiner, Nelson "had a great enthusiasm for the job. He was a tremendous guy to work for."[77]

He also was a realist, a characteristic he refused to hide from his dedicated colony of listeners. "Ralph [Kiner], Bob [Murphy], and I sat down and decided we were going to level and be straightforward; we had a bad club and we had to say so," he said. "And it seemed to work. The Yankees were winners, we were losers."[78]

In semi-retirement Nelson taught his craft to students at his alma mater, the University of Tennessee, then slipped into ill health. When he died in 1995 from Parkinson's disease, an infirmity he had suffered with for years, he was widely regarded as one of the finest sports announcers of all time. His litany of awards confirms that and includes membership in the National Sportswriters and Sportscasters Hall of Fame, the American Sportscasters Hall of Fame, and the New York Mets Hall of Fame; he has also been the recipient of the Baseball Hall of Fame's Ford C. Frick Award, and an Emmy Award for lifetime achievement. The University of Tennessee baseball field—Nelson was the school's first play-by-play announcer—is named, appropriately, Lindsey Nelson Stadium.

Ralph Kiner

My interview with the ailing Kiner just two months before he died may have been his last, and at age ninety-one he could not recall either Paciorek or his accomplishment. When told of Paciorek's feat and asked what he would tell him if the two were ever to meet, Kiner was matter-of-fact: "You will always be recognized as [having done something no one else ever did]," he said. Despite his deteriorating health, Kiner remained a member of the Mets' broadcast team until his dying day. When death finally came from natural causes it put a punctuation mark on the storied life of the Hall of Fame slugger, who had schmoozed with the likes of Frank Sinatra and Bob Hope and romanced leading ladies such as Elizabeth Taylor and Janet Leigh.[79] Gone at last was the notion that Kiner would remain in the broadcast booth forever, as some probably wanted to believe. For the first time since Paciorek's minor-league days Kiner was absent from the Mets broadcast team.

Perhaps Kiner's death gave Paciorek a gift. With the slugger gone, the onetime one-game wonder can look back with a deeper appreciation for the only big-league game he was given, knowing that life and baseball are both finite. Indeed, the former major leaguer—he was irrevocably that—learned an important truth, one that Kiner's passing and his own short career underscored: Forever is never promised . . . and neither is tomorrow.

> *I venture to say that there are millions of adults who would give almost anything to have been a major-league ballplayer for just a day.*
> —*Charlie Grimm, manager*

Appendix

The author's article on John Paciorek, which appeared in the *Los Angeles Times* on January 31, 1991, and introduced his single-game achievement to the world:[80]

John Paciorek Was 3 for 3 in His 1963 Debut, But He Never Played in Another Major League Game

By Steven K. Wagner
Special to *The Times*

Each spring, John Paciorek remembers.

He remembers a sweltering autumn day in 1963. He remembers a Colt Stadium crowd in Houston that cheered his every move, both at the plate and in the field. And he remembers his own performance, one that might never be matched.

That day, 18-year-old John Paciorek made baseball history. On Sept. 29, 1963, during the final game of the season, Paciorek—in his major league debut—stroked three singles, drove in three runs and scored four times for the Houston Colt .45s. He also walked twice, made two fine running catches, and showed Manager Harry Craft—whose club finished in ninth place in the National League—there was reason for optimism in 1964.

In all, Paciorek—the brother of former Dodger Tom Paciorek—went three for three. He had, it turned out, a career day. Literally.

That game, a 13–4 victory over the New York Mets, was the only major league game in which Paciorek would play. He left baseball with a "lifetime" batting average of 1.000—and the finest all-around one-game "career" in major league history.

Each spring, when ballparks from Palm Springs, Calif., to Vero Beach, Fla., are teeming with excitement, John Paciorek, now 45, remembers. And he wonders what might have been.

Why did Paciorek drift into baseball obscurity—and immortality—after that brilliant debut? Interviewed in San Gabriel, where he now lives, Paciorek said a chronic back condition deteriorated after the 1963 season. Though he was invited to spring training the next season, severe pain limited Paciorek's success and forced him to undergo back surgery. He never again reached the major leagues.

Even so, no one can take away The Game.

"It was like a dream—I couldn't believe it was happening," said Paciorek, who is billed as a "one-day wonder" in the 1990 *Guinness Book of World Records*. "I don't know why, but everything seemed to slow down when I faced major league pitching."

Paciorek's major league career can be traced to 1962. Born and raised in Detroit, he earned high school All-American honors in baseball, basketball and football.

In 1962, during his senior year at St. Ladislaus High, Paciorek signed a contract with the Colt .45s, later to become the Astros.

General Manager Paul Richards had high hopes for the 6-foot-2, 210-pound Paciorek. During the 1963 spring training camp Paciorek "hit everything in sight." In an effort to nurture his development, Richards, who died in 1986, sent Paciorek to the club's Class-A team in Modesto, where he played well until suffering the back injury that ultimately would end his career. His intensity and obsession for exercise exacerbated the injury, hastening his departure from baseball.

"I was always hustling," said Paciorek, now a teacher. "I would sprint on and off the field. I would back up everybody. I played very much like Pete Rose even before Rose became known for it. I didn't do it for show— I always wanted to be the best I could be."

The season began with a disappointed Paciorek in Modesto ("I wanted to be like Al Kaline—I didn't want to spend a day in the minors.") and the Colts struggling. As the months passed, the Colts slid deeper into the second division. At the same time, Paciorek's physical problems—he also developed a chronically sore throwing arm—worsened. So did his hitting.

With one game left on the schedule, manager Craft—in an effort to preview his young talent—decided to field a starting lineup that featured eight rookies, including Morgan, Jim "the toy cannon" Wynn, Staub and Zachary. Despite his slump, Paciorek—hurting but still hustling—was selected to start in right field.

"They asked me if I wanted to play, and I said 'yeah,'" Paciorek said.

And play he did. He lined a single down the third base line, a single between shortstop and third base, and bounced a third single deep into the hole. It seemed that every time the 3,899 fans in attendance cheered, Paciorek was either scoring or driving in a runner.

"I don't remember any interviews after the game, but the next day my name was plastered all over the news," he said. "They said, 'This guy's here to stay.'"

In its account of the game, the *New York Times* wrote that Paciorek "found nothing difficult about the majors," adding, "[He] doesn't yet know what it's like to make an out in the big leagues."

The only person not surprised by his performance was Paciorek, who received a standing ovation before his final at-bat.

"I had hit way over .300 in spring training," Paciorek said. "I always thought I belonged [in the big leagues]."

Of the eight rookies who started, only Paciorek and the shortstop Vaughan never played again. The others, including Murrell and Bateman, had long careers.

The next season, Paciorek returned for spring training. Still hurting, he couldn't hit or throw effectively and the Colts sent him back to the minors.

"I was terrible," he said of his 1964 spring training performance. "I did nothing."

By midseason, Paciorek had undergone back surgery.

He spent 10 months in a back brace, then bounced around the minor leagues until Houston released him in 1967.

"They gave me every opportunity to make the team," he said. "They bent over backward for me."

The Cleveland Indians invited him to spring training in 1968, sent him back to the minors, then released him in 1969. Paciorek's baseball career was over.

Tom Paciorek, now a broadcaster for the Chicago White Sox, called the short duration of his brother's major league career "sad."

"He was much better than I was," said the younger Paciorek, who spent 18 years in the major leagues. "He could have had a long major league career."

John Paciorek views his unusual big league career more philosophically than plaintively.

"It's kind of a dubious honor," he said. "But I guess I'm immortalized. I did something no one else has ever done."

Perhaps the Houston Post said it best in its account of the game. In conferring upon Paciorek "the unofficial major league batting title," the newspaper waxed prophetic.

"The rest of [Paciorek's] career," it declared, tongue in cheek, "may be an anticlimax."

Box Score, Houston Colts vs. New York Mets,
September 29, 1963[81]

Mets	ab	r	h	rbi		Colt .45s	ab	r	h	rbi
Kranepool rf	5	0	1	1		Vaughan ss	2	0	0	0
Carmel cf	3	0	0	0		Runnels ph	0	0	0	1
Hunt 2b	3	0	2	0		Farrell p	2	0	0	0
Harkness 1b	3	1	1	0		Dickson p	1	0	0	0
Hickman 3b	4	1	1	0		Morgan 2b	2	1	0	0
Schreiber 3b	0	0	0	0		Wynn lf	3	0	1	2
Hicks lf	4	0	0	0		Staub 1b	4	1	1	1
Coleman c	2	1	1	1		B Aspmte 3b	4	3	2	1
Cannizzaro c	2	0	0	0		Murrell cf	5	1	1	0
Moran ss	2	0	0	0		Paciorek rf	3	4	3	3
Fernandez ph	2	0	0	0		Bateman c	3	2	2	3
Bearnarth p	2	1	2	2		Adlesh ph-c	1	0	0	0
Bauta p	0	0	0	0		Zachary p	1	0	0	0
Stallard p	0	0	0	0		Umbricht p	0	0	0	0
Thomas ph	1	0	0	0		Spangler ph	1	0	1	0
Powell p	0	0	0	0		Lillis ss	2	1	2	2
Smith ph	1	0	1	0						

Team	1	2	3	4	5	6	7	8	9/	R	H	E
Mets	0	0	1	3	0	0	0	0	0/	4	9	2
Colts	0	2	0	5	4	1	1	0	x/	13	13	2

Mets	ip	h	r	er	bb	so
Bearnarth (L, 3–8)	3.0	6	7	7	3	5
Bauta	1.1	4	3	3	1	1
Stallard	0.2	1	1	1	3	1
Powell	3.0	2	2	2	4	1

Colt .45s	ip	h	r	er	bb	so
Zachary	3.1	5	4	4	1	3
Umbricht (W, 4–3)	0.2	1	0	0	0	1
Farrell	3.0	2	0	0	1	1
Dickson	2.0	1	0	0	0	0

John Paciorek's Complete Major-League History[82]

Season	Team	League	AB	H	HR	RBI	BA
1963*	Houston	National	3	3	0	3	1.000

Additional: Runs: 4; OB %, 1.000; Ch, 2; Fld %: 1.000

John Paciorek's Complete Minor-League History[83]

Season	Team	League	Level	BA	HR	RBI
1963	Modesto	California	A	.219	9	49
1964	Durham	Carolina	A	.155	4	12
1964	Statesville	Western Carolinas	A	.063	0	1
1965	Inactive (injured)					
1966	Batavia	NY–Penn	A	.158	3	21
1966	Salisbury	Western Carolinas	A	.247	3	20
1967	Asheville	Carolina	A	.128	1	2
1967	Cocoa	Florida St.	A	.050	0	0
1968	Reno	California	A	.275	17	65
1968	Rock Hill	Western Carolinas	A	.225	3	8

Pitches per At-Bat for John Paciorek

First at-bat (2nd inning): foul, ball, ball, ball, foul, ball
Second at-bat (4th inning): ball, single
Third at-bat (5th inning): ball, ball, called strike, single
Fourth at-bat (6th inning): swinging strike, ball, ball, ball, foul, ball
Fifth at-bat (8th inning): called strike, ball, swinging strike, ball, single

Totals: 23 pitches, 3 singles, 13 balls, 3 foul balls, 2 swinging strikes, 2 called strikes

Aubrey Epps's Complete Major-League History[84]

Season	Team	League	AB	H	HR	RBI	BA
1935*	Pittsburgh	National	4	3	0	3	.750

Additional: R, 1; OB %, .750; PO, 6; E, 2; Fld %: .750

Ken Hubbs's Complete Major-League History[85]

Season	Team	League	AB	H	HR	RBI	BA
1961	Chicago	National	28	5	1	2	.179
1962	Chicago	National	661	172	5	49	.260
1963	Chicago	National	566	133	8	47	.235

Jim Umbricht's Complete Major-League History[86]

Season	Team	League	W	L	SO	ERA
1959	Pittsburgh	National	0	0	3	6.43
1960	Pittsburgh	National	1	2	26	5.09
1961	Pittsburgh	National	0	0	1	2.70
1962	Houston	National	4	0	55	2.01
1963	Houston	National	4	3	48	2.61

Stan Musial's Complete Major-League History[87]

Season	Team	League	AB	H	HR	RBI	BA
1941	St. Louis	National	47	20	1	7	.426
1942	St. Louis	National	467	147	10	72	.315
1943	St. Louis	National	617	220	13	81	.357
1944	St. Louis	National	568	197	12	94	.347
1945	Inactive (military service)						
1946	St. Louis	National	624	228	16	103	.365
1947	St. Louis	National	587	183	19	95	.312
1948	St. Louis	National	611	230	39	131	.376
1949	St. Louis	National	612	207	36	123	.338
1950	St. Louis	National	555	192	28	109	.346
1951	St. Louis	National	578	205	32	108	.355
1952	St. Louis	National	578	194	21	91	.336
1953	St. Louis	National	593	200	30	113	.337
1954	St. Louis	National	591	195	35	126	.330
1955	St. Louis	National	562	179	33	108	.319
1956	St. Louis	National	594	184	27	109	.310
1957	St. Louis	National	502	176	29	102	.351
1958	St. Louis	National	472	159	17	62	.337
1959	St. Louis	National	341	87	14	44	.255
1960	St. Louis	National	331	91	17	63	.275
1961	St. Louis	National	372	107	15	70	.288
1962	St. Louis	National	433	143	19	82	.330
1963	St. Louis	National	337	86	12	58	.255

Final-Game Statistics for John Paciorek, Stan Musial, Ken Hubbs, and Jim Umbricht, September 29, 1963

Player	AB	R	H	RBI	BB	SO	P	A
Paciorek rf	3	4	3	3	2	0	2	0
Musial lf	3	0	2	1	0	1	0	0
Hubbs 2b	3	0	0	0	0	0	1	4

Pitcher	IP	H	R	ER	BB	SO	HR
Umbricht W(4–3)	0.2	1	0	0	0	1	0

National League Players Who Competed in Their Final Regular-Season Game on September 29, 1963[88]

Marv Breeding, Los Angeles Dodgers
Alex Grammas, Chicago Cubs
Gene Green, Cincinnati Reds
Joe Hicks, New York Mets
Ken Hubbs, Chicago Cubs
Stan Musial, St. Louis Cardinals
Charlie Neal, Cincinnati Reds
Bob Oldis, Philadelphia Phillies
John Paciorek, Houston Colt .45s
Grover Powell, New York Mets
Carl Sawatski, St. Louis Cardinals
Frank Torre, Philadelphia Phillies
Jim Umbricht, Houston Colt .45s
Glenn Vaughan, Houston Colt .45s
Ken Walters, Cincinnati Reds

American League Players Who Competed in Their Final Regular-Season Game on September 29, 1963[89]

Tom Brown, Washington Senators
Mike Joyce, Chicago White Sox
Brian McCall, Chicago White Sox

Acknowledgments

In his epilogue to *Stan Musial: An American Life*, author George Vecsey noted that because of a bad experience the ballplayer had encountered stemming from an earlier biography penned by someone else, "I was told I would not get to meet Musial while I was working on [the] book."[90] Fortunately, I had better luck with **John Paciorek**.

Because his 148 minutes of fame occurred more than half a century ago it was clear from the outset that three elements would be necessary in order for me to satisfactorily complete this book: cooperation from John himself, interviews with his brothers and his surviving former teammates, and success tracking down an audiotape of his perfect game.

Throughout the process John's input, including his willingness to sit for lengthy interviews, was invaluable. Without his support the myriad details of his life and brief career that are contained on these pages would have been impossible to collect. Many thanks to John for his beyond-the-call assistance and tireless cooperation.

I am also grateful to the dozens of people, mostly ballplayers, broadcasters, and even an umpire, who were willing to share their stories with me, including recollections of having played with John in the Arizona Instructional League, at the Colt .45s' minor-league training camp, at Modesto, and, ultimately, with the Houston Colt .45s. Interviews with former players from many walks of life helped me to understand and better convey the impact their interactions had on John's life as well as on their own lives.

Essential to framing John's unique story was the audiotape, a broadcast originally recorded by the New York Mets. Acquiring it proved to be a worthy challenge, since the game was played half a century ago and involved two teams battling it out on the final day of a regular season that both franchises probably wished to forget.

My research began with **Bob Hulsey**, caretaker of a Houston Astros fan site called AstrosDaily.com. Hulsey noted that **Pat Rispole** of Schenectady, New York, had recorded many New York Mets and other major-league games over a period of years; after he died in 1979 his estate sold the recordings to **John Miley**, a collector who in turn donated them to the **Library of Congress**. **Andy Holden**, owner of Baseball Direct, which sells rare baseball broadcasts and films, provided me with contact information for Miley, who lives in Indiana, and I called him. Miley told me he had indeed acquired Rispole's vast collection (reportedly for $10,000), now known as The Miley Collection, and donated it to the Library of Congress in 2011. With that my search shifted from the Hoosier State to Washington, DC, and the vaunted Library itself.

A big thanks goes to the Library's **Brian Cornell**, with the Recorded Sound Department; **Jerry Hatfield**, in the Public Service Office, Motion Picture, Broadcasting, and Recorded Sound Division; and **David Sager**, with the Recorded Sound Reference Center, also in the Motion Picture, Broadcasting, and Recorded Sound Division, who collectively navigated me through the necessary governmental red tape and provided me with a digital version of the game audio, which Rispole had originally recorded using reel-to-reel technology.

Thanks also to **Colin Dwyer**, who as a Georgetown University graduate student graciously assisted me by listening to the tape at the Library of Congress, a prerequisite to the Library digitizing the audio for my use. Dwyer, now a writer himself, was referred to me by *Dr. Kathryn Temple*, chair and associate professor in the busy Department of English at Georgetown. I am deeply appreciative of her efforts in making time to find a student willing to assist me with this labor of love.

The vast majority of statistical information contained on these pages was provided by several sources: the *Baseball Encyclopedia*, Baseball-Reference.com, Retrosheet, and the *Baseball Almanac*. It would be impossible to footnote each reference, and I am grateful to each for compiling this data.

A special thank-you to the late *Ralph Kiner*, who consented to an interview when his health was failing shortly before his death, as well as *Lindsey Nelson* and *Bob Murphy*, who also are deceased. The trio's clear depiction of the twenty-three pitches thrown to John on that memorable day was instrumental in making this book happen.

Due to the lack of eyewitness corroboration, certain nonessential statements are assumed to be correct: an umpire's stance, a batter's mannerisms, a player's thoughts at a particular moment, et cetera. In each instance such actualizations are believed to have occurred based upon the historical record and the author's knowledge of baseball.

Finally, my heartfelt thanks goes to my daughter, *Hannah*, a great source of encouragement and herself a fine writer, and my wife, *Michelle*, who supported this project when at times it seemed I should have been working on less speculative ventures.

I would be remiss if I failed to acknowledge one more person. Working behind the scenes throughout the process, incorporating all phases of the project with great skill, was *Garth Battista*, publisher of Breakaway Books. His willingness to take on a new author is greatly appreciated, and his steady hand at the Breakaway wheel is the sole reason this book came to fruition.

Toward the end of his literary effort that portrayed Musial's life Vecsey unexpectedly crossed paths with Stan the Man at the Missouri Athletic Club, where Musial had frequently dined and was cherished; the two were introduced and politely shook hands before Musial was wheeled away by a grandson to his usual table. To his credit, John offered me much more than a handshake, warmly welcoming me into his home and his place of work on several occasions. The rest of the story, written on these pages, is, unmistakably, baseball history.

—SKW

Notes

1. Nicholson, George W. "The Branch Rickey Award." The Branch Rickey Award, n.d. Web. Accessed July 26, 2013. http://www.branchrickeyaward.org/branch-rickey-by-justice-george-nicholson.
2. "Willie Stargell Quotes." Baseball Almanac, n.d. Web. Accessed August 3, 2013. http://www.baseball-almanac.com/quotes/quostar.shtml.
3. Paciorek, John F. *The Principle of Baseball: And All There Is to Know About Hitting.* Bloomington, IN: Balboa, 2012, p. 66. Print.
4. Ibid., p. 1.
5. Brown, David. "Twenty Questions with John Paciorek." *Northwest Herald* [Chicago], September 17, 2006. Print.
6. Wagner, Steven K. "It's All in Day's Work." *Los Angeles Times*, January 31, 1991, pp. C1–C11. Print.
7. Elston, Gene. 09/26/08—"One-Game Gamers." AstrosDaily.com, n.d. Web. Accessed July 26, 2013. http://www.astrosdaily.com/column/10809260117fan.html.
8. Tiemann, Bob, and Andy Singer. "First National Association Game." Retrosheet, n.d. Web. Accessed July 30, 2013. http://www.retrosheet.org/1stGame.htm.
9. Babwin, Don. "Woman Who Shot Baseball Player and Inspired Movie Dies at 83." Associated Press, March 17, 2013. Print.
10. Wagner, Steven K. "It's All in Day's Work." *Los Angeles Times*, January 31,1991, pp. C1–C11. Print.
11. "About Hamtramck." City of Hamtramck, n.d. Web. Accessed July 26, 2013. http://hamtramck.us/about/index.php.
12. Detroit Tigers, n.d. Web. Accessed July 26, 2013. http://detroit.tigers.mlb.com/index.jsp?c_id=det.
13. "Tom Paciorek." Baseball-Reference.com, n.d. Web. Accessed July 26, 2013. http://www.baseball-reference.com.
14. "Records in Little League Play." Little League, n.d. Web. Accessed July 26, 2013.
15. "Former Major Leaguer Tells of Abuse by Michigan Priest." Associated Press, March 22, 2002. Print.
16. Ibid.

17. Ibid.

18. Bradlee, Ben. *Kid: The Immortal Life of Ted Williams*. N.p.: Little Brown, 2013, p. 74. Print.

19. Keith, Ted. "The Perfect Game." *Sports Illustrated*, July 9, 2012. Web. Accessed July 26, 2013. http://sportsillustrated.cnn.com/vault/article/magazine/MAG1201779/index.htm.

20. Wagner, Steven K. "It's All in Day's Work." *Los Angeles Times*, January 31, 1991, pp. C1–C11. Print.

21. "An Interview with John Paciorek." Interview by Thomas Wayne. Dugout Central, 2009. Web. Accessed July 26, 2013. http://www.fannation.com/blogs/post/202564.

22. Paciorek, John F. *The Principle of Baseball: And All There Is to Know About Hitting*. Bloomington, IN: Balboa, 2012, p. 19. Print.

23. Ibid.

24. Reichler, Joseph L. "The Development of Baseball." In *The Baseball Encyclopedia*, 7th ed. New York: Macmillan, n.d., pp. 9–12. Print.

25. Walsh, Volney. "Aubrey Epps Gets Trial Next Spring." *Pittsburgh Press*, September 2, 1934. Print.

26. "Young Catcher Is Fighting for Life at Memphis." Associated Press, October 31, 1935. Print.

27. Balinger, Edward F. "Four Weeks in Texas Camp." *Pittsburgh Post-Gazette*, December 31, 1935. Print.

28. Sandomir, Richard. "Lindsey Nelson, 76, Broadcaster for Mets for 17 Years, Is Dead." *New York Times*, June 12, 1995. Print.

29. Hillman, John. "Baseball's Perfect Hitters." *Baseball Research Journal* 26–27 (1997), p. 102. Print.

30. Nelson, Sarah. "A Baseball Rookie Scores Big on Life's Playing Field." Christian Science JSH Online, April 2004. Web. Accessed July 26, 2013. http://jsh.christianscience.com.

31. "Colt Stadium." BallparksOfBaseball.com, n.d. Web. Accessed July 26, 2013. http://www.ballparksofbaseball.com/past/ColtStadium.htm.

32. Ibid.

33. Coyne, Larry, and David Dietz. "Stan Musial's Last Game." *St. Louis Post-Dispatch* 14 Feb. 2011: n. pag. Print.

34. Dickerson, Larry. "From Readers: On Stan Musial's Last Game, Larry Dickerson Tagged Along." *Columbia Missourian* 23 Jan. 2013: n. pag. Print.

35. Paciorek, John F. *The Principle of Baseball: And All There Is to Know About Hitting*. Bloomington, IN: Balboa, 2012, p. 200. Print.

36. Ibid., p. 69.

37. "Baseball Star Is Killed." *News and Courier* [Charleston, SC], February 16, 1964, pp. 1–2A. Print.

38. Murray, Jim. "The Pride of Colton." *Los Angeles Times*, April 28, 1964. Print.

39. Gutsky, Earl. "Memories of Ken Hubbs Live On: Nearly 30 Years Later, the Town of Colton Still Is Recovering from His Death at 22." *Los Angeles Times*, July 5, 1993. Print.

40. Reisner, Alex. "Baseball Geography and Transportation." *Baseball Research Journal* 35 (2007), p. 46. Web. Accessed July 26, 2013. http://sabr.org/content/baseball-research-journal-archives.

41 Ibid.

42. Ibid.

43. "Too Tragic to Believe—Cubs Brass." *Independent Press* [Long Beach, CA], February 16, 1964, p. C1. Print.

44. Rosetta, Dick. "Remembering 1960s Cubs Second Baseman Ken Hubbs." *Salt Lake Tribune*, February 14, 1994. Print.

45. Looney, Jack, and Chicago Cubs. "Cubs Uniform Numbers." CubsByTheNumbers.com, n.d. Web. Accessed July 26, 2013. http://www.cubsbythenumbers.com/cubsuni.html.

46. Vanderberg, Bob. "Best of the Cubs by Uniform Number." *Chicago Tribune*, March 29, 2009. Print.

47. "Hubbs' Death Brought Sorrow to Southland." *Los Angeles Times*, February 13, 1999. Print.

48. Smith, Curt. *Voices of the Game: The First Full-Scale Overview of Baseball Broadcasting, 1921 to the Present*. South Bend, IN: Diamond Communications, 1987. Print.

49. "National Cancer Institute." National Cancer Institute, n.d. Web. Accessed July 26, 2013. www.cancer.gov/cancertopics/ types/melanoma.

50. "Jim Umbricht Dead; Pitcher on Colts, 33." *New York Times*, April 8, 1964. Print.

51. Ibid.

52. "Colts to Wear Black Arm Bands for Jim Umbricht." *The Day* [New London, CT], April 9, 1964, p. 26. Print.

53. "Baseball Almanac." Baseball Almanac, n.d. Web. Accessed July 26, 2013. http://www.baseball-almanac.com/feats/feats10n.shtml.

54. Wynn, Jimmy, and Bill McCurdy. *Toy Cannon: The Autobiography of Baseball's Jimmy Wynn*. Jefferson, NC: McFarland, 2010, p. 91. Print.

55. Ibid.

56. "Leukemia Fatal to Walter Bond." *Observer-Reporter* [Washington, PA], September 15, 1976. Print.

57. "Jim Umbricht Dies of Cancer." *Pittsburgh Press*, April 8, 1963, p. 56. Print.

58. "Baseball Card." Cartoon. New York: Topps Chewing Gum, 1963. Print.

59. "John Paciorek: One-Game Wonder." Interview by Andrew J. Kahn. Andrewjkahn.com, September 30, 2011. Web. Accessed July 26, 2013. http://andrewjkahn.com/2011/09/30/john-paciorek-one-game-wonder.

60. "Harry Craft, Mantle's First Manager, 80." *New York Times*, August 5, 1995. Print.

61. Keith, Ted. "The Perfect Game." *Sports Illustrated*, July 9, 2012. Web. Accessed July 26, 2013. http://sportsillustrated.cnn.com/vault/article/magazine/MAG1201779/index.htm.

62. "An Interview with John Paciorek." Interview by Thomas Wayne. Dugout Central, 2009. Web. Accessed July 26, 2013. http://www.fannation.com/blogs/post/202564.

63. Ibid.

64. Nelson, Sarah. "A Baseball Rookie Scores Big on Life's Playing Field." Christian Science JSH Online, April 2004. Web. Accessed July 26, 2013. http://jsh.christianscience.com.

65. Keith, Ted. "The Perfect Game." *Sports Illustrated*, July 9, 2012. Web. Accessed July 26, 2013. http://sportsillustrated.cnn.com/vault/article/magazine/MAG1201779/index.htm.

66. "Young Colts Route Mets." Associated Press, September 30, 1963. Print.

67. Wagner, Steven K. "It's All in Day's Work." *Los Angeles Times*, January 31, 1991, pp. C1–C11. Print.

68. "An Interview with John Paciorek." Interview by Thomas Wayne. Dugout Central, 2009. Web. Accessed July 26, 2013. http://www.fannation.com/blogs/post/202564.

69. Ibid.

70. Ibid.

71. Ibid.

72. "John Paciorek: One-Game Wonder." Interview by Andrew J. Kahn. Andrewjkahn.com, September 30, 2011. Web. Accessed July 26, 2013. http://andrewjkahn.com/2011/09/30/john-paciorek-one-game-wonder.

73. Tellis, Richard. *Once Around the Bases: Bittersweet Memories of Only One Game in the Majors*. Chicago: Triumph, 1998, p. 239. Print.

74. Ibid., p. 241.

75. "Stan Musial." National Baseball Hall of Fame, n.d. Web. Accessed August 2, 2013. http://baseballhall.org.

76. Sandomir, Richard. "Lindsey Nelson, 76, Broadcaster for the Mets for 17 Years, Dies." *New York Times*, June 12, 1995. Print.

77. Ibid.

78. Smith, Curt. *Voices of the Game: The First Full-Scale Overview of Baseball Broadcasting, 1921 to the Present*. South Bend, IN: Diamond Communications, 1987. Print.

79. Madden, Bill. "Ralph Kiner, Mets Broadcasting Legend and Hall of Fame Pirates Player, Dead at 91." *New York Daily News*, February 6, 2014. Print.

80. Wagner, Steven K. "It's All in Day's Work." *Los Angeles Times*, January 31, 1991, pp. C1–C11. Print.

81. Baseball-Reference.com, n.d. Web. Accessed July 26, 2013. http://www.baseball-reference.com/boxes/HOU/ HOU196309290.shtml.

82. Ibid., http://www.baseball-reference.com/players/p/paciojo01. shtml.

83. "John Paciorek: The Greatest One Game Career in Major League History." *Astroland: The Anteroom*. Astroland.net, n.d. Web. Accessed July 26, 2013. http://www.astroland.net/paciorek.html.

84. Baseball-Reference.com, n.d. Web. Accessed July 26, 2013. http://www.baseball-reference.com/players/e/eppsau01.shtml.

85. Ibid., http://www.baseball-reference.com/players/h/hubbske01.shtml.

86. Ibid., http://www.baseball-reference.com/players/u/umbriji01.shtml.

87. Ibid., http://www.baseball-reference.com/players/m/musiast01.shtml.

88. "1963 National League Retirements." Baseball-Almanac.com, n.d. Web. Accessed July 26, 2013. http://www.baseballalmanac.com/yearly/final.php?y=1963&l=NL.

89. Ibid.

90. Vecsey, George. "Epilogue." *Stan Musial: An American Life*. New York: Ballantine, 2011, p. 336. Print.

Index

Photo by Hannah E. Wagner

STEVEN K. WAGNER has worked as a freelance journalist since 1989. The author began his career with the *Monmouth Sun-Enterprise* in Oregon and later worked for the *Oregon City Enterprise-Courier* and the *Portland Daily Journal of Commerce* before joining United Press International as a staff writer in Boise, Idaho. He also worked for the *Portland Oregonian* as its Vancouver, Washington, bureau chief and as the newspaper's night crime reporter. Mr. Wagner has freelanced extensively for the *Los Angeles Times* and his work also has appeared in the *New York Times*, *Oklahoma City Oklahoman*, *Seattle Times*, *Baseball America*, and numerous other newspapers and magazines. He is married, has two grown children, and currently resides in Claremont, California.